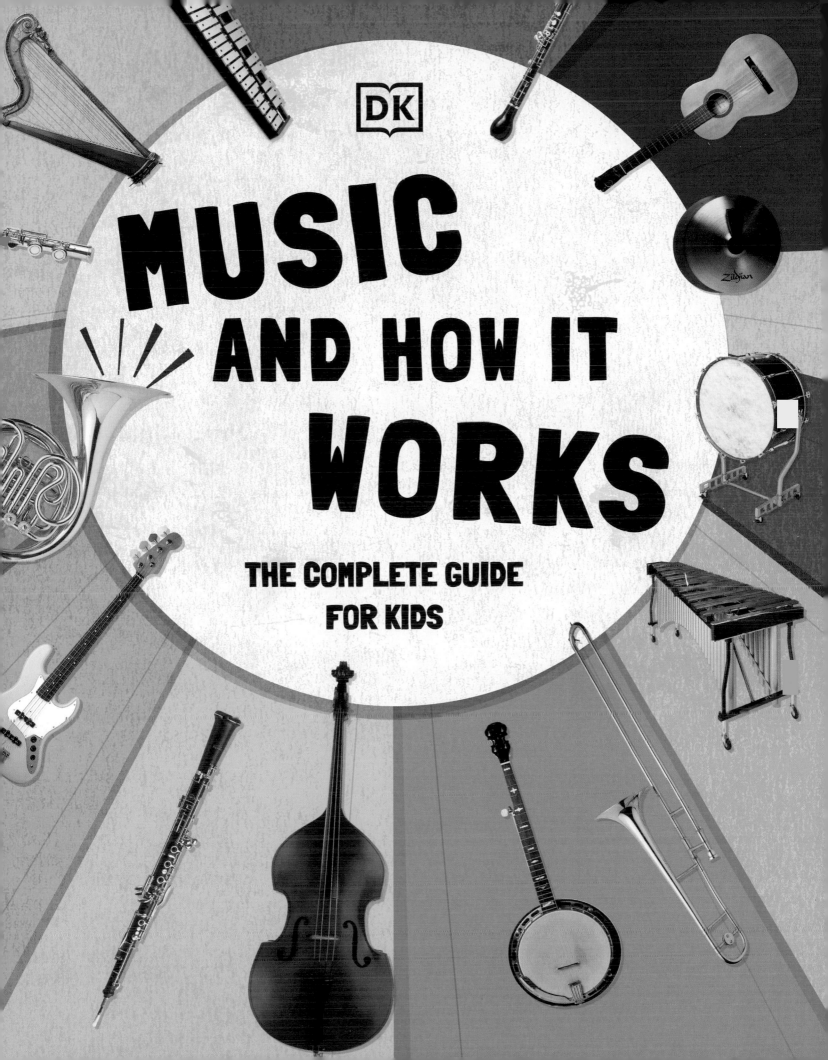

MUSIC
AND HOW IT
WORKS

THE COMPLETE GUIDE
FOR KIDS

CONTENTS

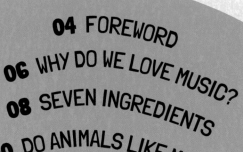

https://spoti.fi/3cuBfps

FEATURE PLAYLISTS

The best way to learn about music is to listen! To find the playlists in this book, ask a grownup to help you scan this code using a cellphone. Or, search for the songs online!

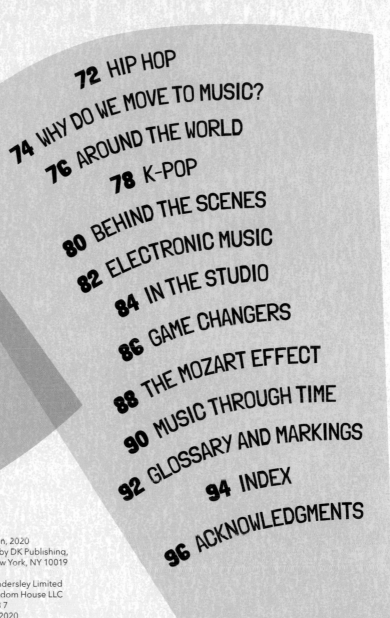

DK | Penguin Random House

Written by Charlie Morland
Illustrated by David Humphries
Consultant Gareth Dawson
Editor Kat Teece
US Editor Karyn Gerhard
US Senior Editor Shannon Beatty
Lead Designer Clare Baggaley
Project Art Editor Victoria Palastanga
Project Editor Kritika Gupta
Senior Designer Nidhi Mehra
Senior Commissioning Designer
Fiona Macdonald
DTP Designers Sachin Gupta,
Vijay Kandwal
Managing Editors Jonathan Melmoth,
Monica Saigal
Managing Art Editors
Diane Peyton-Jones,
Romi Chakraborty
Project Picture Researcher
Sakshi Saluja
Production Editor Dragana Puvacic
Production Controller John Casey
Jackets Coordinator Issy Walsh
Delhi Team Head Malavika Talukder
Publishing Manager Francesca Young
Creative Director Helen Senior
Publishing Director Sarah Larter

First American Edition, 2020
Published in the United States by DK Publishing,
1745 Broadway, 20th Floor, New York, NY 10019

Copyright © 2012 Dorling Kindersley Limited
DK, a Division of Penguin Random House LLC
23 24 25 10 9 8 7
018–316571–Nov/2020

A catalog record for this book is available
from the Library of Congress.
ISBN: 978-1-4654-9990-5

DK books are available at special discounts
when purchased in bulk for sales promotions,
premiums, fund-raising, or educational use. For
details, contact: DK Publishing Special Markets,
1745 Broadway, 20th Floor, New York, NY 10019
SpecialSales@dk.com

Printed and bound in China

For the curious
www.dk.com

MIX
Paper | Supporting
responsible forestry
FSC™ C018179

This book was made with Forest
Stewardship Council™ certified
paper—one small step in DK's
commitment to a sustainable future.
For more information go to
www.dk.com/our-green-pledge

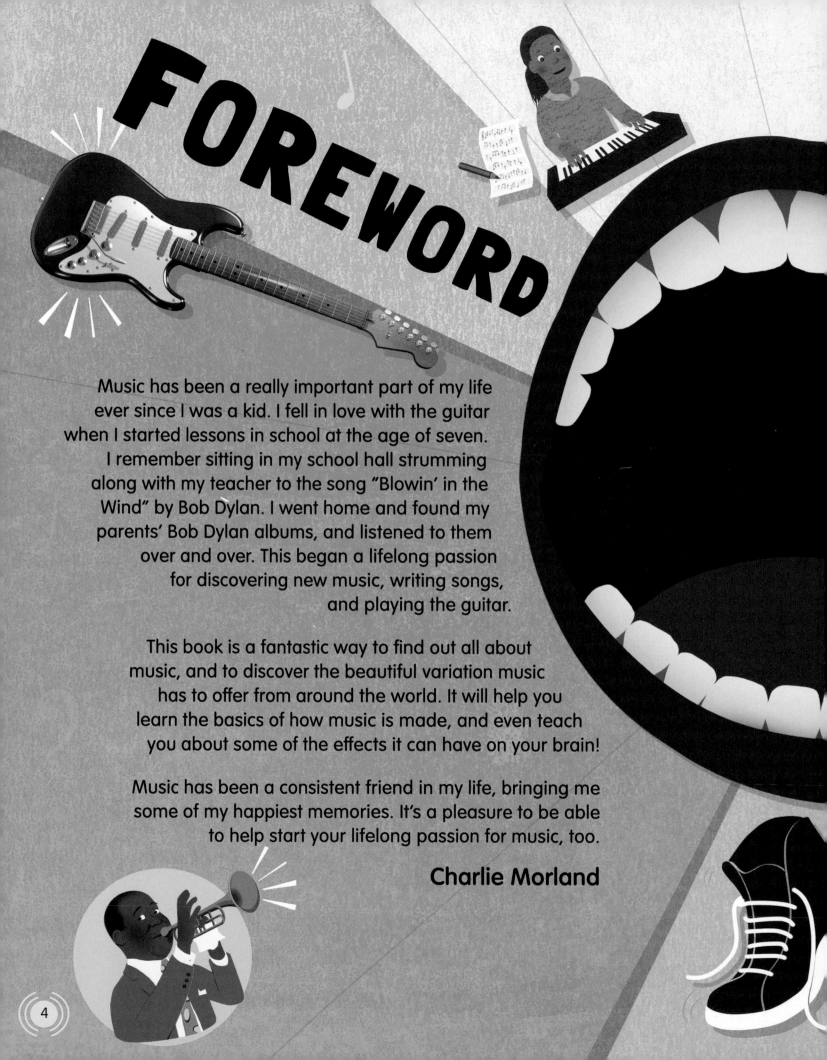

FOREWORD

Music has been a really important part of my life ever since I was a kid. I fell in love with the guitar when I started lessons in school at the age of seven. I remember sitting in my school hall strumming along with my teacher to the song "Blowin' in the Wind" by Bob Dylan. I went home and found my parents' Bob Dylan albums, and listened to them over and over. This began a lifelong passion for discovering new music, writing songs, and playing the guitar.

This book is a fantastic way to find out all about music, and to discover the beautiful variation music has to offer from around the world. It will help you learn the basics of how music is made, and even teach you about some of the effects it can have on your brain!

Music has been a consistent friend in my life, bringing me some of my happiest memories. It's a pleasure to be able to help start your lifelong passion for music, too.

Charlie Morland

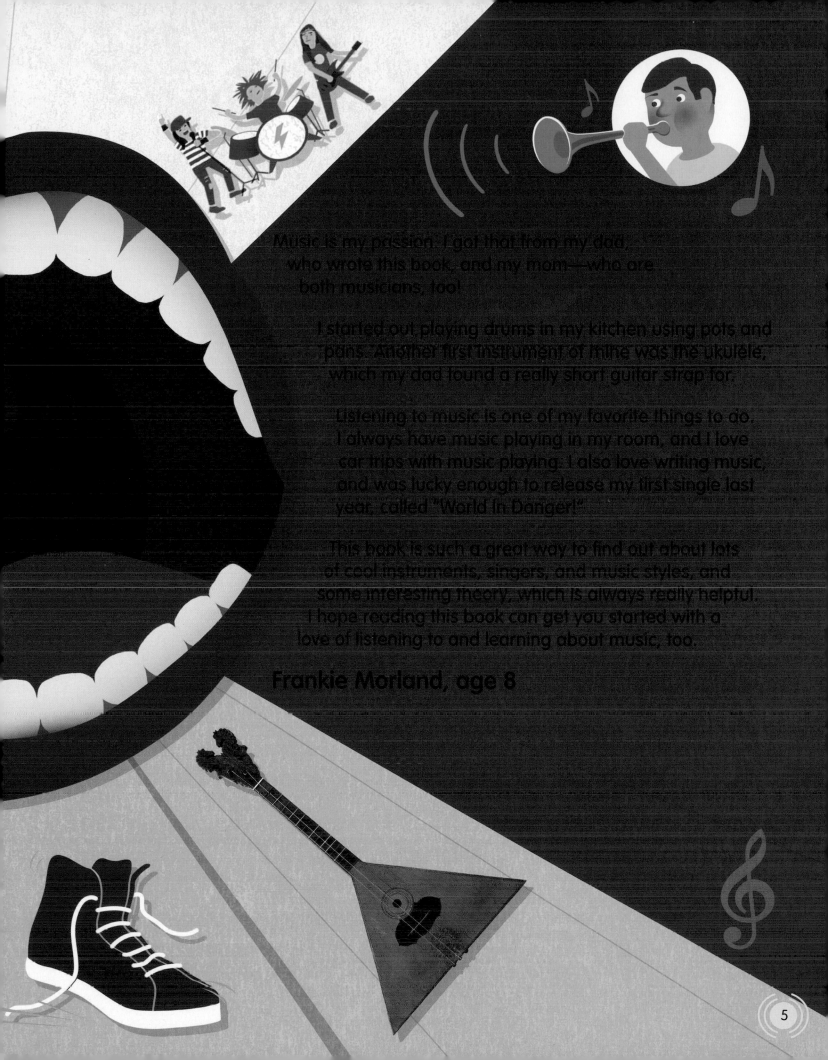

Music is my passion. I got that from my dad, who wrote this book, and my mom—who are both musicians, too!

I started out playing drums in my kitchen using pots and pans. Another first instrument of mine was the ukulele, which my dad found a really short guitar strap for.

Listening to music is one of my favorite things to do. I always have music playing in my room, and I love car trips with music playing. I also love writing music, and was lucky enough to release my first single last year, called "World in Danger!"

This book is such a great way to find out about lots of cool instruments, singers, and music styles, and some interesting theory, which is always really helpful. I hope reading this book can get you started with a love of listening to and learning about music, too.

Frankie Morland, age 8

WHY DO WE LOVE MUSIC?

Whether you're dancing to music at a party or relaxing to it in your room, listening to music is a powerful act. It can improve your mood or make you feel sad, and it can even help you remember things from the past.

THE PLEASURE PART

Scientists have looked at the brain to see how listening to music affects it. They found that music activates a part of the brain that makes us feel pleasure, called the limbic system. This system is active when we do other pleasurable things, such as eating tasty food.

Limbic system

Dopamine pathway

HAPPY CHEMICAL

A chemical called dopamine is released in the limbic system when we listen to music. Dopamine travels along pathways in the brain to make us feel good.

PUZZLING IT OUT

Pop artist Taylor Swift

When you listen to music, your brain tries to work out what sounds will come next, like a puzzle. We find this enjoyable because our minds love figuring out the answers to puzzles!

A NICE DISTRACTION

Concentrating on music can distract you from other things that are going on. This might make you feel better if you're upset or annoyed.

Danish poster for *The King of Jazz* (1930)

OLD MEMORIES

We often remember songs better than speech. We feel emotion when we listen to music, which helps create stronger memories. Songs contain rhyming words and other memorable features. This means music can help us remember fun moments or times in our lives!

Elderly people can often recall music from their past, such as the soundtracks to old musicals, long after they've forgotten everything else.

MOVING TO THE BEAT

Whether it's a tap of the foot or a backflip, music makes us want to move. Dancing causes our brains to release a mixture of chemicals that brings us enjoyment!

PICKING FAVORITES

Your brain can solve the puzzle of what comes next in a piece of music the more you listen to that style of music. This means that your favorite genre (style) is probably the one you're most familiar with!

ALL THE FEELS

Listening to music doesn't just make us happy. If you like being creeped out by ghost stories, you might enjoy music that makes you feel scared, such as the soundtrack to a spooky film. If you're sad, you might want to listen to music that matches how you feel.

Pop artist Beyoncé and rapper Jay-Z

A hummed tune is a melody. Tap your foot regularly and you've got a rhythm. These are both ingredients of music. There are seven main ingredients that can be put together in different ways, either all together or a few at a time.

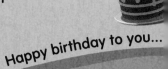

Happy birthday to you...

Happy birthday to you...

SEVEN INGREDIENTS

RHYTHM

Can you feel your heart beating? This regular beat is a pulse. The pulse of music is called rhythm. Musicians need to know the rhythm to play in time with one another.

Keep the beat
Rhythm is made up of beats. When you tap or stomp your foot to music you are "keeping the beat," or following the rhythm of the music.

DYNAMICS

The volume of music is called dynamics. Music can have loud sections, quiet sections, or even complete silence.

QUIET

LOUD

Amplitude
Sound travels in waves. The louder the sound, the taller the wave. We call this the amplitude.

Scales
A melody can come from a musical scale, which is a set collection of notes.

MELODY

A single musical sound is called a note. It might be sung or played on an instrument. Putting notes in an order creates a melody. Often, the melody is the memorable part of a song, known as the hook.

FORM

When writing music, musicians decide how to structure it, or give it form. The piece could have repeated sections, such as verses and choruses. Or, it might have no repetition at all!

Happy birthday dear reader...

Repetition
The song *Happy Birthday* repeats the same line, but with slightly different notes each time.

Happy birthday to you!

TEXTURE

Music is often made up of multiple instruments playing at the same time. This creates texture. Each instrument creates a layer, such as a guitar melody.

TIMBRE

The same note can be played using a recorder or a trumpet—but it sounds different. Each instrument has a unique quality to it. This is called the instrument's timbre.

Clarinet

Orchestra
The instruments in an orchestra create texture through multiple melodies and harmonies.

Flute

Recorder

Trumpet

Saxophone

HARMONY

More than one note played at the same time creates a harmony. Harmonies can make music sound happy, sad, or scary—and everything in between.

Material difference
The material an instrument is made from, such as brass or plastic, affects the timbre.

Experimenting
In the piece *4:33*, by John Cage, musicians play nothing for 4 minutes and 33 seconds. It seems like this uses no ingredients at all! However, it uses the dynamics of silence, and its length gives it a form.

Choirs
A choir is made up of people singing different notes to build beautiful harmonies.

DO ANIMALS LIKE MUSIC?

From birds in the sky to fish at the bottom of the sea, animals of all shapes and sizes make songlike calls. This is mostly for communication rather than for enjoyment. However, scientists have studied animals to see if they can enjoy human music.

COWS

Cows appear to be more relaxed when listening to music humans find soothing. Experiments have shown that they produce more milk when they listen to soothing songs than when they listen to other types of music.

The humpback whale's songs

Male humpback whales put together different sounds, such as whoops and groans, into repeating patterns to make a song. These songs catch on and are sung by other males, like pop songs.

The songs are probably to attract females.

DOGS

Dogs seem to find reggae music relaxing, like humans do! When scientists played this style of music to pooches they barked less. But they were their normal, bouncy selves with other kinds of music.

Emily Doolittle composed classical pieces based on birdsong.

CATS

Scientists played cats classical music but saw no reaction. However, they made music that matched the pitch of a cat's meow, and found the animals rubbing up against the speakers. This is probably because they recognized the sounds.

FISH

We can tell the difference between pieces of music, but can fish? It seems so! Scientists trained fish to eat only when the classical composer Bach was played. When they played classical music by Stravinsky, the fish didn't eat. They could tell the difference.

THE MUSICAL ALPHABET

Music has its own alphabet of letters, called notes. They can be high or low, and we put them together to make tunes. Learn the notes by playing your very own multicolored paper piano!

SHARPS AND FLATS

You can sharpen a note, which means make it higher in pitch, using a sharp accidental. To flatten a note, which means to lower the pitch, use a flat accidental. Accidental notes are generally found on the black keys.

NOTES

There are seven musical notes. They are named after the first seven letters of the alphabet—A, B, C, D, E, F, and G.

INTERVALS

The movement from one note to another in a scale is called an interval. This movement can be a large jump across many notes, or a small jump to the next note.

\# This symbol means the note is **sharp**.

This symbol means the note is **flat**.

This is an **interval** of five notes, or a fifth.

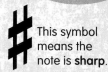

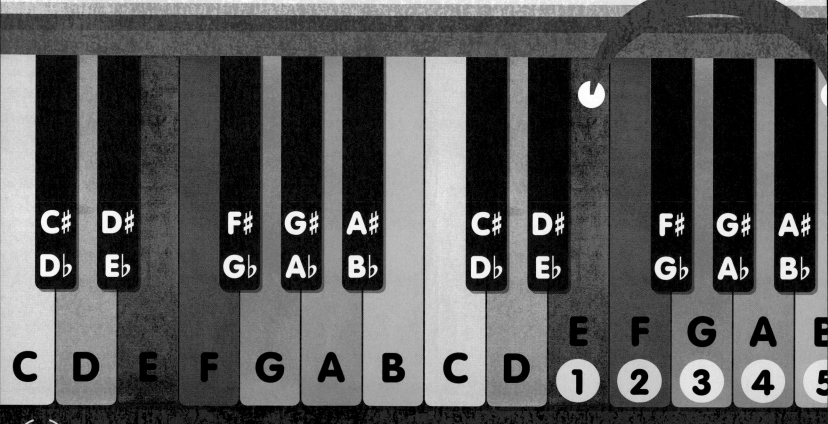

The natural—neither flat nor sharp—notes on a piano are usually white.

WHOLE AND HALF STEPS

Moving one note at a time is known as a half step, or a semitone interval. Moving two notes is known as a whole step, or a tone.

OCTAVES

There are eight natural notes in an octave, which are repeated all the way up the piano keyboard. The octaves get higher as you move from left to right.

Add the name here!

Moving from C to C# is a **half step**.

Moving from D to E is a **whole step**.

Two notes that share the same pitch, such as F# and G♭, are called **enharmonic** notes.

The notes B to C and E to F don't have a black note between them.

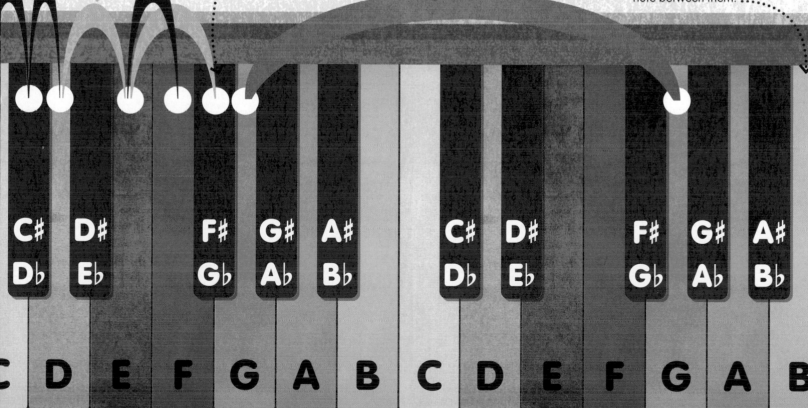

Happy birthday

Can you "play" *Happy Birthday* on the piano? Here are the notes!

G G A G C
Hap-py birth-day to

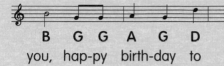

B G G A G D
you, hap-py birth-day to

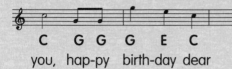

C G G G E C
you, hap-py birth-day dear

B A F F E C D C
........., hap-py birth-day to you!

PERCUSSION

A percussion instrument, such as a drum, is something that's hit or scraped to create sound. The beat of these instruments helps everyone else in a band play at the same speed. The percussion layer of music is also called the groove.

HOW IT WORKS

Playing a percussion instrument causes the surface to vibrate. This creates vibrations in the air called sound waves. The harder the instrument is hit, the louder the sound.

The cymbal vibrates when hit.

Crash cymbal

High tom

Hi-hat

Snare drum

Bass drum

HI-HAT

The hi-hat is made up of two cymbals on top of each other. The drummer can close them together or open them up to change the sound using a foot pedal.

XYLOPHONE

The wooden bars of a xylophone are hit with a mallet (a stick with a ball on the end). The shorter the bars are, the higher sound they make.

TAMBOURINE

Pairs of metal tines line the tambourine's frame. These jingle against one another when the instrument is shaken or hit with the player's palm.

SNARE DRUM

The snare drum has a short, sharp, snapping sound. It is generally played on beat three of the bar.

RIDE CYMBAL

This large cymbal is often used in the chorus instead of a hi-hat to create a variety of sounds.

Ride cymbal

CHIMES

The metal tubes in a set of chimes create a sound that gets gradually higher, when played from long to short, or lower, when played from short to long.

Middle tom

TOM-TOM

There are usually three toms in a drum set, played using drumsticks. These are tuned, or adjusted, to make high to low-pitched sounds.

Floor tom

GONG

Gongs make deep, booming noises when hit. They are often used to create an impressive ending to a piece.

BASS DRUM

Played with a foot pedal, the bass drum gives a deep thud. It is often played on beat one of a bar.

Human percussion

You can make all sorts of percussion sounds with your body. Try clapping your hands, snapping your fingers, stomping your feet, or clicking your tongue. Can you think of any pieces of music that use human percussion sounds?

TRADITIONAL AFRICAN STYLES

Each country in Africa has its own distinctive style of music. However, elements reappear between styles, such as complex drum parts. Traditional music plays a similar role in each society, used for community events such as celebrations.

Call and response

In call and response music, a group leader makes a call that is answered by the other members together. This answer is called the chorus. The leader can improvise, but the chorus remains the same.

Chorus

Leader

THE MBIRA

This Zimbabwean instrument is a wooden box with metal strips, called tines, attached. Each tine plays a certain pitch, according to its length. The instrument is played by plucking the tines with your thumb.

TIMELINE

c.6000–4000 BCE
People paint a dance scene on a cave wall, showing how important music and dancing is to them.

c.1000 BCE
Mbiras with metal tines are invented, replacing bamboo or wood tines.

Polyrhythms

Polyrhythms are common in African drum music. This is when two or more different rhythms are played together at the same time, to create interesting rhythmic textures.

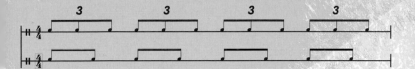

PLAYLIST

1. Solomon Vandy – **African Children's Choir**
2. Hello My Baby – **Ladysmith Black Mambazo**
3. Tribal Dances Music – **African Tribal Drums**
4. Gambia – **Sona Jobarteh**
5. African Drums – **African Tribal Orchestra**

Celebrations for a new king in Benin

Celebrations

In some African communities, music is performed during traditional celebrations and ceremonies. People join in by singing, clapping, and dancing along.

South-African singing group, Ladysmith Black Mambazo

Paul Simon

Influence

African music helped shape many modern styles. Blues and jazz were developed by African Americans, inspired by elements such as call and response. Paul Simon worked with African musicians on his pop album, *Graceland*.

1100s CE The djembe drum is thought to have been invented by the Mandinka tribe, in what is now Mali, in West Africa.

1600s CE Enslaved people are transported from Africa to be sold abroad, taking their music styles with them.

Slave ship

HOW IS SOUND MADE?

Music comes from vibrations that travel through the air. These can be caused by strings on a guitar, a column of air inside a trumpet, or vocal cords—folds of skin inside your throat that vibrate when you speak.

TINY VIBRATIONS

A sound is made when something vibrates. The vibration causes air particles to move in a wave. If this reaches your ear, it moves to the brain and is converted into a sound.

Sound waves
The vibrating drum skin causes the air to vibrate in a wave.

Vibration
The wave moves through the air.

Drum
The drum skin vibrates when it is hit.

THE BRAINY BIT

A particular part of your brain, called the auditory cortex, tells you what you're hearing.

Auditory cortex
Your brain has two halves, each with its own auditory cortex.

Vestibulocochlear nerve

Particles that vibrate quickly create a high-pitched sound.

INTO YOUR HEAD

The wave causes different parts of the inner ear to vibrate. The vibrations are changed into a signal, which a nerve carries to the brain. The brain then tells you what you're hearing—whether it's a drum beat or a human voice.

Ear canal
The wave travels through this passage.

Vestibulocochlear nerve This carries the signal to the brain.

Middle-ear bones
These tiny bones vibrate to pass the sound along.

Eardrum
This thin sheet of tissue vibrates due to the wave.

Auditory tube
A tube connects the mouth and ear.

To the throat

Cochlea
Hairlike cells on this swirling structure pick up the vibrations, which are changed into a signal for the brain.

Vibrations in action
Speech can travel along string stretched between two paper cups. When the string is pulled tight, talking into one of the cups passes the sound vibration along the string to the other cup.

Earlobe
The outer ear directs the wave into the inner ear.

HOW TO BUILD A SONG

When it comes to writing your first song it can be hard to know where to start! Songwriting is an art form, and like all art there are lots of different styles and techniques. Luckily, there are songwriting structures to follow, such as the classic pop–song arrangement shown here.

INTRO

The introduction, or intro, is important because it's the first thing listeners hear, and you want them to like the song right away! It's usually four bars long, and instrumental.

VERSE ONE

This is often the first section of singing. Verses tell most of the story of the song, and each one is different. A verse can be any length, but usually is eight bars long, and gets louder as it transitions into the chorus.

CHORUS

The chorus is the catchy part. It's usually about eight bars long, louder than the earlier sections, and will have more layers to make it stand out. Each chorus in a song tends to be the same.

Paul Simon
The verses in *You Can Call Me Al* begin with the same line. Can you hear it?

Dire Straits
Money For Nothing has a memorable intro, and contains a guitar-riff hook.

HOOK

This is the part that sticks in your head and makes you want to listen again. The hook can be melodic or rhythmic. Great songs will have a hook in the intro and chorus.

PLAYLIST

1. Money For Nothing – **Dire Straits**
2. You Can Call Me Al – **Paul Simon**
3. Life On Mars? – **David Bowie**
4. Yellow Submarine – **The Beatles**

OUTRO

Songs can end with an outro section that sometimes fades to nothing.

BRIDGE

This breaks up the song's repetitive structure. It might add something new, such as a different chord progression, rhythm, or lyric. It builds into the final chorus, and tends to be about eight bars long.

VERSE TWO

The second verse often has the same melody and length as verse one, with different lyrics.

CHORUS

FINAL CHORUS

The final chorus is often the most impressive part of a song. It can be louder, use more instruments, or have more powerful vocals.

PRE-CHORUS

Some songs have a pre-chorus, which links each verse to the chorus. It might be instrumental, or an excitement-building vocal part.

David Bowie
Listen for the memorable pre-chorus in *Life On Mars?*.

The Beatles
Yellow Submarine has a memorable chorus about a colorful underwater home.

CLASSICAL

Musicians train for many years to perform complicated classical pieces, often alongside other musicians in orchestras. Composing this kind of music requires lots of skill, too. There can be many parts to think of, and it needs to be written down for musicians to follow.

THE ORCHESTRA

The orchestra is a combination of instruments from different families, with as many as 100 musicians all performing together! Leading it is the conductor, who keeps everyone in time by signaling with a stick called a baton.

Orchestral instruments
The instruments in an orchestra can vary. However, you'll often find the ones shown here.

Xylophone

Trumpets

French horns

Cymbals

Oboes

Flutes

Second violins

Violas

First violins

Conductor

TIMELINE

RENAISSANCE ERA (1450–1600) Vocal choral music is popular, as well as music from new instruments such as the viol.

Viol

BAROQUE ERA (1600–1730) New forms appear, such as the concerto, for a soloist accompanied by an orchestra.

Baroque composer Antonio Vivaldi

Yuja Wang

The grand piano

The grand piano is an important part of many orchestras. Pressing a key causes a hammer to strike a string inside the body. This can create a loud or a soft sound, controlled by foot pedals.

Dynamics

Volume can be changed in a piece to make it more exciting. It might build from a softly played section to a loud, energetic part. These shifts in volume, called dynamics, are noted in the score with special markings.

Very loud	*ff*	Fortissimo
Loud	*f*	Forte
Medium loud	*mf*	Mezzo-forte
Medium soft	*mp*	Mezzo-piano
Soft	*p*	Piano
Very soft	*pp*	Pianissimo

Dynamic marking

Chamber music

Chamber music is performed by small groups. Each musician has their own part to play. This differs from orchestral music, in which a group of musicians might play the same part.

Timpani

Trombones

Gong

Tuba

Double basses

Bassoons

Cellos

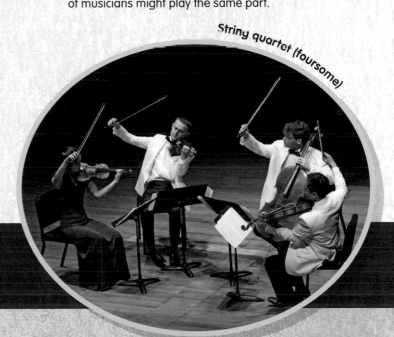
String quartet (foursome)

CLASSICAL ERA (1750–1830)
Melody is important in compositions, the piano grows popular, and woodwinds become common in orchestras.

18th-century piano

ROMANTIC ERA (1830–1900)
Passionate operas and shorter pieces are written, inspired by other art forms.

Romantic composer Frédéric Chopin

INDIAN CLASSICAL

Indian classical music sounds very different from the classical music that began in Europe. It features creative rhythms, small intervals between the notes, and improvisation. It also has its own interesting instruments.

SPIRITUAL CONNECTION

Indian classical musicians often feel a deep spiritual connection with their music. Improvised pieces of music may last for longer than an hour.

North and south

North Indian classical music is known as Hindustani. It is based on improvisation and the raga (see opposite). South Indian classical music is called Carnatic. Its pieces are shorter and more structured.

↑ Hindustani
Carnatic ↓

Drone

A drone is a constant note played under a piece of music. In Indian classical music, the drone is usually the root note of the scale used in the piece.

Tanpura

This completely hollow, stringed instrument creates the drone note.

Kaushiki Chakraborty

TIMELINE

1500–1200 BCE
Sacred Hindu songs, known as Vedic hymns, are passed down orally through the generations.

India

1300s Indian classical music begins to divide into two broad types—Hindustani in the north and Carnatic in the south.

Hindustani pioneer Tansen

Sa Re Ga Ma Pa Dha Ni Sa

Raga

The raga refers to various musical scales, each with its own feel or mood. Musicians play different ragas at different times of the day; they are also associated with different seasons and occasions.

Bilāwal is the basic raga scale used in Hindustani.

▶ PLAYLIST

1. Dhun – **Ravi Shankar (Hindustani)**
2. Sadra in Sankara Karan – **Ali Akbar Khan (Hindustani)**
3. Alaipayuthe Kanna – **Aruna Sairam (Carnatic)**
4. Sriramachandra – **T.M Krishna & Sangeetha Sivakumar (Carnatic)**

Tabla

This pair of small drums is widely used in Indian classical music. The different sounds each drum creates are given names, such as Nā, Tin, and Tun. Playing the two drums together creates even more sounds.

The smaller drum is called the dayan. It is played with the dominant hand.

Ravi Shankar

This famous sitar player has helped popularize Indian classical music around the world. He has also inspired many Western musicians to learn and study it.

The larger drum is called the bayan.

1969 Ravi Shankar plays the Woodstock music festival. He introduces the sitar to many people around the world, including George Harrison of the Beatles.

Woodstock

2000s The songs used in Indian, or Bollywood, films begin to fuse Indian classical music and Western pop, creating a new genre.

Indian composer A. R. Rahman

25

CLASSICAL COMPOSERS

Talented classical composers bring all the parts of a piece together in jaw-dropping ways. Their work can be powerful enough that people still listen to it hundreds of years later. Here are just a few classical geniuses from history.

ANTONIO VIVALDI (1678-1741)

An Italian composer, Vivaldi was a virtuoso violinist. In his twenties, he taught violin and wrote music at the Ospedale della Pietá, an orphanage and music school in Venice, Italy. He went on to compose several operas, and was inspired by the weather for a famous set of instrumental works called *The Four Seasons*.

JOHANN SEBASTIAN BACH (1685-1750)

Born in Germany, Johann spent some of his teenage years playing the organ for churches. He began composing music for the organ, as well as for other instruments. He wrote in multiple forms, and used clever patterns in his music, such as fugues. Over his entire life, Johann composed more than 175 hours of music! Try listening to *Cello Suite No.1 in G Major*.

FRÉDÉRIC CHOPIN (1810-1849)

Polish composer Frédéric showed talent for playing the piano as a child, and was performing pieces for an audience at the age of eight. By the age of 20, he was composing impressive works. Frédéric's famous compositions were based around the piano. *Nocturne Op.9 No.2* is a great example of his work.

PYOTR ILYICH TCHAIKOVSKY (1840-1893)

Tchaikovsky grew up in Russia and was a talented piano player by the age of eight. When a new music school opened in the Russian city of Saint Petersburg, called the Saint Petersburg Conservatory, he jumped at the chance to attend. Tchaikovsky composed fantastic works for orchestra, including *The Nutcracker*, which includes the famous piece *Dance of the Sugar Plum Fairy*.

CLAUDE DEBUSSY (1862-1918)

This French pianist and composer learned his skills at a world-famous music school in France—the Conservatoire de Paris. Claude's works are often called impressionist, which means they create a mood or atmosphere. He was often inspired by poetry. His most well-known piece is *Clair de Lune*.

BENJAMIN BRITTEN (1913-1976)

Born in England, Benjamin loved music from an early age and was already trying to compose pieces when he was five. As a musically trained adult, he wrote chamber and orchestral pieces, and many operas. *The Young Person's Guide to the Orchestra* is not only a wonderful piece of music, it also explains the orchestra for children.

Players blow across the hole in the mouthpiece.

Keys close holes in the side, changing how air flows through the tube to make the pitch higher or lower.

WIND INSTRUMENTS

FLUTE

Early flutes were wooden tubes, with holes that changed the pitch when covered with fingers. Modern flutes are metal, with keys to cover holes. Flutes often play high-pitched tunes.

Wind instruments are hollow objects that you blow into to create noise. People have been using them for thousands of years. Today, there are two main types—brass and woodwind.

WOODWIND

CLARINET

This single-reed instrument can play a wide range of notes, making it a popular choice in many different genres of music.

How reeds work

Some woodwind instruments have a thin piece of wood in the mouthpiece, called a reed. The player blows across the reed, making it vibrate. Double-reed instruments have two reeds that vibrate together.

Bite plate

Bore

Vibrating reed

Woodwind mouthpiece

BASSOON

The bassoon is a double-reed instrument. The tubing of a bassoon is coiled up because it is 9.8 ft (3 m) long—much taller than an adult man!

OBOE

The double-reed oboe can produce a clear, bright sound. This helps it stand out when played in an orchestra.

HOW IT WORKS

The musician blows air into or across a mouthpiece. This creates a vibrating column of air inside the instrument, which makes a sound that comes out of the other side. Different shaped tubes make different sounds. Valves or keys can be opened or closed to change the pitch.

Mouthpiece magic
The air inside brass instruments is made to vibrate by blowing through pursed lips.

Breath

Vibrating column of air

BRASS

FRENCH HORN

Modern horn instruments get their names from animal horns, which were hollowed and used as instruments in ancient times. If the French horn tubing was unwrapped it would be up to 18 ft (5.5 m) long!

TUBA

The tuba is the lowest-pitched brass instrument. It is also the largest—often around 3.5 ft (1 m) high, or about the size of a small child.

Valve

TRUMPET

The trumpet plays the highest pitch of all the valved brass instruments. It is popular in jazz as well as classical music.

Slide
An extra section of tube can be slid into place.

SAXOPHONE

Although made of brass, the saxophone is a woodwind instrument because it has a reed. It uses keys to change the notes, like a woodwind instrument.

TROMBONE

The trombone uses a sliding section rather than valves to change the tubing length, so it can change pitch very smoothly.

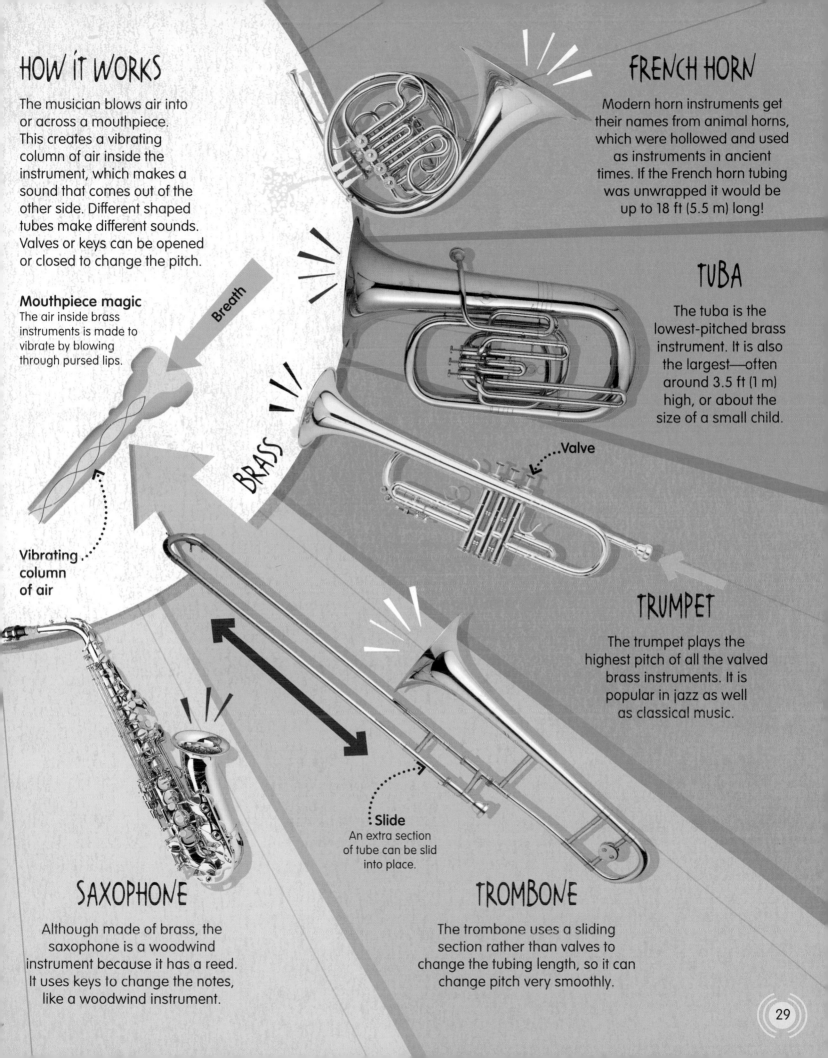

READING MUSIC

Whether you're playing a famous tune or making up a new one, it helps to be able to read and write music. For this, we use a staff, made of five horizontal lines. Each note sits on a line, or in the space above or below lines.

Made-up words or phrases called mnemonics can help you remember notes.

TREBLE CLEF

The treble clef, also known as the G clef, circles around the second-from-bottom line on the staff. This line represents the note G, with the rest of the notes in order around it.

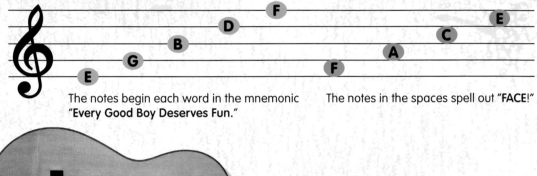

The notes begin each word in the mnemonic **"Every Good Boy Deserves Fun."**

The notes in the spaces spell out **"FACE!"**

Treble range
The treble clef is used for playing higher notes. Guitar music is usually written in the treble clef.

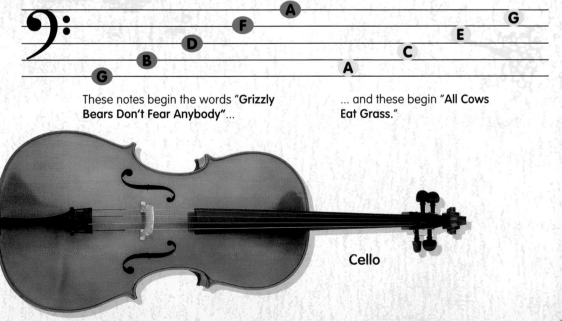

Acoustic guitar

BASS CLEF

The notes in the bass-clef range are lower in pitch than those in the treble-clef range. The bass clef is also known as the F clef. It has two dots that sit above and below the second-from-the-top line on the staff. This line represents the note F.

These notes begin the words **"Grizzly Bears Don't Fear Anybody"**...

... and these begin **"All Cows Eat Grass."**

Bass range
The bass clef is usually used for cello music.

Cello

TYPES OF NOTES

A written note not only indicates whether a pitch is high or low, it also tells musicians how long to play the sound. Some notes are long, while others are short. Written music also tells musicians when to not play a note, by using markings called rests.

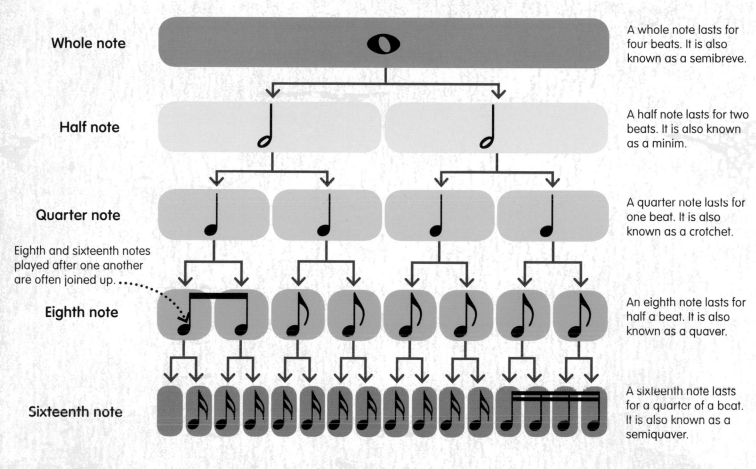

Whole note

A whole note lasts for four beats. It is also known as a semibreve.

Half note

A half note lasts for two beats. It is also known as a minim.

Quarter note

A quarter note lasts for one beat. It is also known as a crotchet.

Eighth and sixteenth notes played after one another are often joined up.

Eighth note

An eighth note lasts for half a beat. It is also known as a quaver.

Sixteenth note

A sixteenth note lasts for a quarter of a beat. It is also known as a semiquaver.

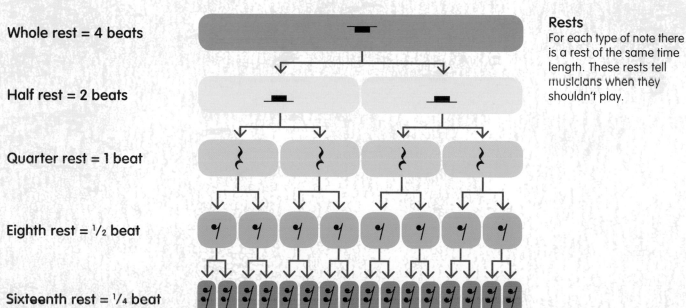

Whole rest = 4 beats

Rests
For each type of note there is a rest of the same time length. These rests tell musicians when they shouldn't play.

Half rest = 2 beats

Quarter rest = 1 beat

Eighth rest = ½ beat

Sixteenth rest = ¼ beat

OPERA

The best operas have the audience in tears—either from sadness or laughter! Operas use music to tell a story, with characters singing about how they feel. The singers are highly trained, and their voices soar above classical music played by an orchestra.

Singing sensations

Do you have what it takes to be an opera singer? You'll need powerful vocals to fill theaters, the ability to hit a wide range of notes across multiple octaves, and have a beautiful tone.

Jessye Norman

The opera house

Traditional opera houses are grand, gold-painted theaters. There are velvet curtains ready to draw across the stage, plush audience seating in rows or in high-up, private boxes, and a pit in front of the stage for the orchestra.

TIMELINE

1607 *L'Orfeo* is written by Claudio Monteverdi. It is now seen as the first operatic masterpiece, and is still often performed.

A scene from *L'Orfeo*

1637 The first public opera house opens in Venice, Italy. It shows *L'Andromeda* by Francesco Manelli.

Teatro San Cassiano

Singing ranges

There are many different opera ranges, including the ones below.

Soprano is the highest range, and is usually sung by a female.

Alto is one of the lowest female ranges.

Tenor is a medium range, and usually the highest a male can sing.

Bass is the lowest singing range, sung by men.

▶ PLAYLIST

1. Nessun Dorma – **Luciano Pavarotti**
2. O mio babbino caro – **Katherine Jenkins**
3. L'amour est un oiseau rebelle – **Maria Callas**
4. Libiamo ne' lieti calici – **Placido Domingo**
5. The Flower Duet – **Kiri Te Kanawa and Katherine Jenkins**

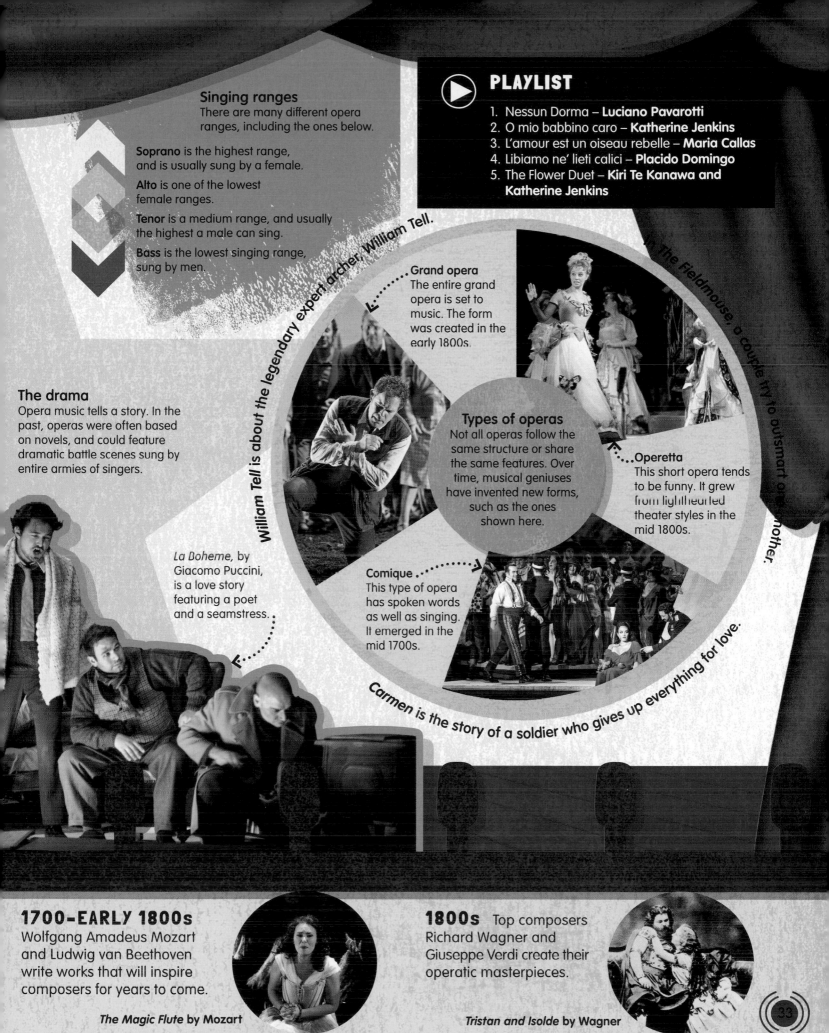

William Tell is about the legendary expert archer, William Tell.

...in the Fieldmouse, a couple try to outsmart one another.

The drama

Opera music tells a story. In the past, operas were often based on novels, and could feature dramatic battle scenes sung by entire armies of singers.

Grand opera

The entire grand opera is set to music. The form was created in the early 1800s.

Types of operas

Not all operas follow the same structure or share the same features. Over time, musical geniuses have invented new forms, such as the ones shown here.

Operetta

This short opera tends to be funny. It grew from lighthearted theater styles in the mid 1800s.

La Boheme, by Giacomo Puccini, is a love story featuring a poet and a seamstress.

Comique

This type of opera has spoken words as well as singing. It emerged in the mid 1700s.

Carmen is the story of a soldier who gives up everything for love.

1700–EARLY 1800s

Wolfgang Amadeus Mozart and Ludwig van Beethoven write works that will inspire composers for years to come.

The Magic Flute by Mozart

1800s
Top composers Richard Wagner and Giuseppe Verdi create their operatic masterpieces.

Tristan and Isolde by Wagner

HOW HIGH CAN YOU GO?

Can you sing higher than your friends? What about your parents? It depends on your vocal range—the distance between the lowest note and the highest note you can sing. Some animals can sing much higher than we can, or roar much lower.

Trachea

Vocal cord

Tongue

VOCAL CORDS

The vocal cords, or folds, vibrate as air from the lungs passes through them, creating a sound. The longer the vocal folds, the slower the vibration and the deeper the voice.

BLACKPOLL WARBLER

Birds can produce higher notes than humans. They have two sets of tiny vocal flaps that vibrate very quickly.

UP TO c.10,000 HZ

Sound is measured in hertz (Hz)—the higher the number of Hz, the higher the sound.

UP TO c.1,046 HZ

SOPRANO

Children have shorter, still-growing vocal cords, which vibrate quickly to create high-pitched sounds. Most children can sing the highest vocal range—soprano. This range is usually sung by women in operas.

UP TO c.698 HZ

ALTO

Women's vocal ranges are higher than men's. This is because they tend to have shorter vocal cords. The highest female range is soprano, alto falls in the middle, and contralto is the lowest range.

UP TO c.200 HZ

LION

Lions have large, stretchy, square-shaped vocal folds that vibrate slowly to create a very deep noise. Their roar helps them to scare off other lions.

UP TO c.330 HZ

BASS

Men's voices tend to be deeper than those of women and children, because men usually have longer vocal folds. The lowest male vocal range is bass.

DOLPHIN

Up to c.150,000 Hz that are too high for humans to hear. Instead of vocal cords, they have nose. The lips that project into the nose. The lips vibrate when air pushes past them, causing the passage to vibrate and produce a sound.

Dolphins can produce sounds called structures called vocal cords. The lips project into the nose. The lips vibrate when air pushes past them, causing the passage to produce a sound.

FOLK

Throughout time, ordinary people have wanted to tell their stories through song. These songs developed into different types of folk music around the world. American and British folk music share similar instruments, such as the fiddle and the acoustic guitar.

Woody Guthrie
Popular American folk musician Woody Guthrie was first taught folk music by his father. His songs told tales about everyday life in the countryside of Oklahoma.

ORAL ROOTS

Most early folk songs weren't written down—they were passed down orally, or by mouth. People in communities sang the same songs through the centuries. Stories and songs that are passed down in this way are called folklore. People began to write the songs down in the 1800s.

SCARBOROUGH FAIR

No one knows who made up the British folk song *Scarborough Fair,* or when. It is thought to have been changed over hundreds of years as it was passed down orally.

TIMELINE

MID 1800s William Thoms comes up with the term "folklore." He and others like him write down the stories and songs passed down orally.

LATE 1800s New technology, such as the phonograph, allows folk songs to be recorded and played back.

19th-century phonograph

The fiddle

Folk musicians call the violin "the fiddle." This name sets it apart from violins in classical music, because the style of playing tends to be different. Fiddle music often uses lots of fast, short notes intended to get people dancing!

Sam Sweeney, from the folk band Bellowhead

▶ PLAYLIST

1. The Sound of Silence – **Simon and Garfunkel**
2. Where Have All the Flowers Gone – **Pete Seeger**
3. Devil's Spoke – **Laura Marling**
4. Light Flight – **Pentangle**
5. Ho Hey – **The Lumineers**

This strumming pattern is down, down, up.

Folk guitar

How you play a guitar changes the sound and feel of the music. Folk musicians will either strum chords using a plectrum—a small piece of plastic held by the fingers—or pick the strings in a style known as "fingerpicking."

Modern folk

Folk music today often combines traditional folk elements, such as the fiddle and lyrics about everyday problems, with influences from other modern music styles, such as instruments from pop and rock.

Wildwood Kin

The electric guitar is usually played in rock music.

1962 American artist Bob Dylan releases his first album, which fuses traditional folk with rock to create a new style.

1965 The first Cambridge Folk Festival takes place. This and newer folk music festivals are still popular today, and feature lots of musicians.

Cambridge Folk Festival

BALALAIKA

This Russian instrument has a triangular body and three strings. It comes in both large and small sizes, and it is often played in folk music.

DOUBLE BASS

"Bass" describes a low-pitched sound. The double bass is sometimes called the upright bass because it's played upright, either by plucking or with a bow.

VIOLIN

The violin makes a high-pitched sound. It is usually played with a bow, which is called the arco style of playing. Plucking the strings is known as the pizzicato style.

CELLO

The cello is played in an upright position with a bow or by plucking. It has a low-pitched sound and is usually part of an orchestra, or played in an ensemble with other stringed instruments.

STRING INSTRUMENTS

A string is a great way to create a sound, because the pitch can be easily changed by tightening or loosening it. Stringed instruments come in many shapes and sizes. Let's take a look at some.

GUITAR

Some people play the guitar by strumming it, which means to brush the fingers over every string. The strings can also be plucked.

GUZHENG

The guzheng is a Chinese instrument with 21 strings. It is plucked to make a soothing sound.

The sound box

Stringed instruments often have a hollow chamber, called a sound box, that makes the sound louder. The sound goes from the strings into the sound box and comes out through one or more holes.

English guitar

HARP

Harpists use their fingers to pluck the strings. The lengthy strings create long-lasting notes.

HOW IT WORKS

When a string is played it vibrates. This causes the air particles around it to start vibrating in a wave, allowing the sound to travel to our ears.

SITAR

The Indian sitar's unique sound is created by two types of strings. Some strings are plucked, which disturbs others that make a droning sound.

.... Finger plucking

: Bow

AEOLIAN HARP

This curious instrument from Ancient Greece is played by the wind. A breeze blows across the strings, causing them to vibrate.

Playing methods

Strings can be plucked with a finger, strummed (brushed) with a hand or guitar pick, drawn (moved across) with a bow, hit with hammers, or even set in motion by the wind.

COUNTRY

Country was created in the South by poor workers. Individuals sang about their lives while playing cheap string instruments, such as the guitar. Today, the string instruments and personal tales remain, with country groups singing masterful harmonies.

Simple chords

Traditional country music was mostly made up of simple chords and chord progressions (chords played one after another). These were easy to write and play, as early artists weren't trained musicians.

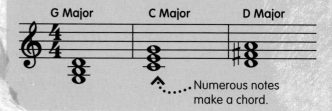

G Major   C Major   D Major

Numerous notes make a chord.

WORKERS' ROOTS

The train was the main form of transportation for the people first creating country music, in the early 1900s. It also provided jobs. This made trains a popular topic for early country music songs!

Many country stars wear rhinestones that glitter when they catch the light.

Dolly Parton

Songwriter Dolly Parton is one of country's most successful artists. Songs such as *Jolene,* which is about a beautiful woman, are famous worldwide.

TIMELINE

EARLY 1920S

John Carson and other workers at cotton mills in Atlanta become some of the first country recording artists.

1937
Hank Williams starts his career. He later becomes one of the genre's most popular artists, known as the "King of Country."

Maggie Björklund

PLAYLIST

1. Ring of Fire – **Johnny Cash**
2. 9 to 5 – **Dolly Parton**
3. Earl's Breakdown – **Earl Scruggs**
4. Guilty – **The Shires**
5. Our Song – **Taylor Swift**

Pedal steel

Country music often features an instrument called a pedal steel. The player moves a bar along the strings, which are stretched lengthways across the top. This creates a smooth movement between notes. A foot-operated pedal also alters the pitch.

Earl Scruggs playing the banjo

MODERN COUNTRY

Country music has changed to include more varied instruments and sounds. It is now more popular than ever, in other countries as well as in the US.

The Shires' album, *Brave*, was the first by a UK country act to make one of the national top 10 best-selling albums of the week.

Banjo

An important instrument in country music, the banjo has a sharp sound that can easily be heard above other instruments. The strings are usually picked, which means pulled with the fingers, in a style called banjo rolls.

The Shires

1955 Johnny Cash records his first songs, starting his journey to become one of country's most well-known names.

2006 Taylor Swift releases her first album, at the age of 16. She later wins one of the biggest prizes in music—the Best Album award at the Grammys—twice.

THE MATH OF MUSIC

If you're a musician, you might have secret math powers, too. Math and music seem like very different topics, but they're actually linked. Musicians are expert at counting beats, and clever composers create patterns.

PATTERNS

Math is full of patterns, which involve using a rule—such as "add ten"—to form a sequence of numbers. Patterns are everywhere in music, too! Canons and rounds are two examples.

COUNTING BEATS

Math is needed to keep to the right speed when playing music. If a bar contains four quarter notes, musicians count in fours so they know when to play a note.

1   2   3   4   1   2   3   4

Canons

A canon is when members of a group sing the same melody, beginning at different times. If the tune repeats, a canon is also called a round, because it goes around and around.

Part 1

Part 2

Fugues

Classical pieces called fugues contain a tune that is repeated. The main tune or theme is known as the subject. It is started by different instruments at different times, often at varying tempos, pitches, and keys.

Music whiz, math genius

Children who play music are more likely to be good at math. Scientists found that musical students tended to score higher in math tests than those who didn't play instruments.

▶ **PLAYLIST**

1. Pyramid Song – **Radiohead** (uses displaced rhythms)
2. Seven Days – **Sting** (uses odd time signatures)
3. Pachelbel's Canon in D – **Johann Pachelbel** (uses a canon structure)
4. Toccata and Fugue in D minor – **Johann Sebastian Bach**
5. Unsquare Dance – **Dave Brubeck** (uses a $^7/_4$ time signature)

DISPLACED RHYTHMS

Some rhythms begin on a different beat of the bar as the music progresses. This is called displacing the beat, and involves careful counting! It's particularly popular in a music style called math rock.

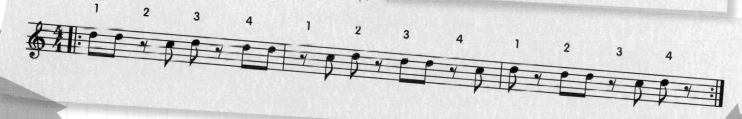

Mirroring

When a shape matches up on either side of a center line, this is called mirroring. One clever way that the composer Bach played with his subject during a fugue was to turn it upside down on the staff, creating a mirror image.

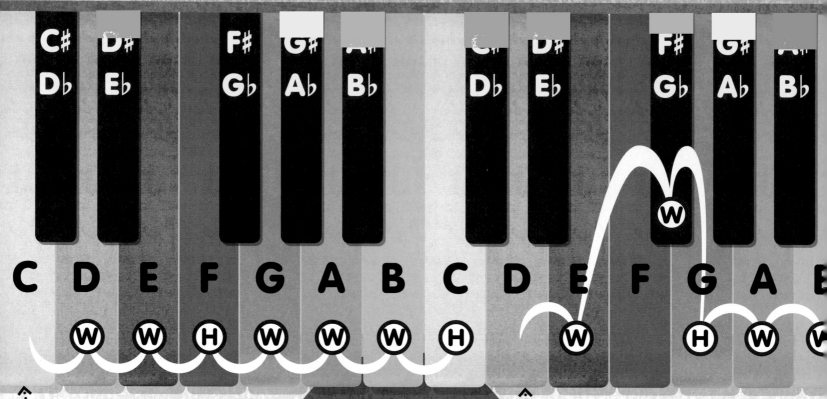

C# Db   D# Eb   F# Gb   G# Ab   A# Bb   C# Db   D# Eb   F# Gb   G# Ab   A# Bb

C D E F G A B C D E F G A B

W W H W W W H — W — H W W

Start here
If we start on C and follow this pattern we create a C major scale.

MAJOR SCALE

One of the most commonly used scales is the major scale. It is always created from the same pattern of intervals—whole step, whole step, half step, whole step, whole step, whole step, half step.

If we start on D and follow the major scale pattern we create a D major scale.

W = Whole note
H = Half note

KEY SIGNATURES

Each key has a unique set of notes that can be identified from its accidentals—its sharps and flats. Writing the sharps or flats at the beginning of a piece tells musicians what key it's in.

INTERVALS

Learn about the different types of intervals on pages 12–13.

The D major key has two accidentals—F# and C#

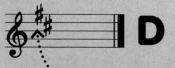

D

The accidentals at the start are called the piece's key signature.

SCALES, CHORDS, AND KEYS

Music is made from notes played individually as a melody, or together as a chord. The melodies and chords in a song come from one or more keys— a set of notes, or pitches.

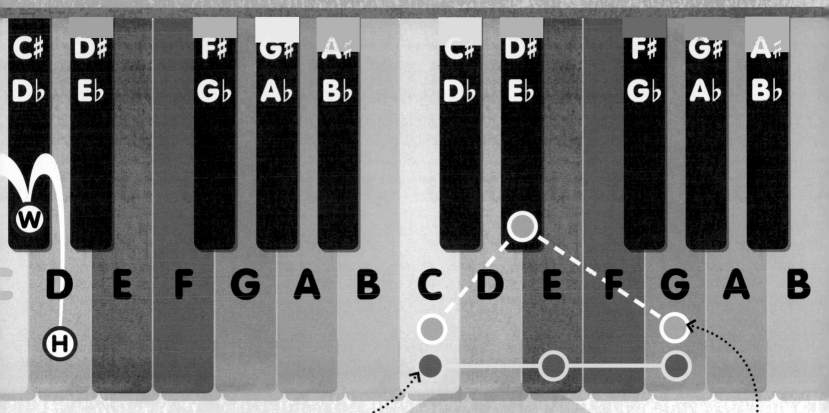

C#/Db **D#/Eb** **F#/Gb** **G#/Ab** **A#/Bb** **C#/Db** **D#/Eb** **F#/Gb** **G#/Ab** **A#/Bb**

D E F G A B C D E F G A B

Playing C, E, and G gives you the C major chord.

Playing C, E flat, and G gives you the C minor chord.

changing the key mid-song adds excitement, and is called a key change.

CHORDS

A chord is the name given to multiple notes played at the same time. Chords containing just three notes are called triads. Let's look at the major and minor triad chords of C.

Major chords
A major triad chord comes from a major scale. The musician plays the first note, called the root, the third note, called the major third, and the fifth note, called the perfect fifth.

Minor chords
Moving the middle note of a major triad down a half step has a big effect on the sound. This new triad is called a minor chord, and has a sad quality to it.

Majorly happy, minorly sad
Usually, major chords sound happy and minor chords sound sad. Train-station announcements often begin with three notes from a major chord, to give a cheerful atmosphere!

THE BLUES

To say "I've got the blues" means "I am feeling sad," which is how this emotional style of music got its name. Early blues featured a solo singer accompanied by a single, soulful instrument, such as a guitar.

Howlin' Wolf

Singing sadness
Traditionally, blues songs are led by emotional vocals, which tell sad stories about hard times. Chicago-born musician Howlin' Wolf once said "any time you're thinking evil, you're thinking the blues."

African American enslaved people in the early 1900s

BLUES BEGINS
From the 1600s to the 1900s, African people were captured, brought to the US, and forced to work as slaves on huge farms. They sang traditional call-and-response songs from their home countries, which meant chanting in a repetitive form. This developed into the 12-bar blues.

Bessie Smith
Singer Bessie Smith was a powerful vocalist nicknamed "the empress of the blues." Bessie had a soulful voice full of emotion, that brought out the sadness in the blues songs she performed.

TIMELINE

LATE 1800s Country blues, sung in the countryside of the South, begins. It is inspired by spiritual songs from enslaved African Americans.

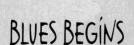

Country-blues star
Robert Johnson (1911–1938)

1920s Bessie Smith releases the track *Downhearted Blues* as a gramophone record. It will go on to sell 2 million copies.

Early 20th-century gramophone

Little Walter

The harmonica
This wind instrument is small, cheap, and easy to carry around, which suited early traveling blues singers. Players can move smoothly from one note to the next, creating emotional melodies.

 PLAYLIST

1. Hoochie Coochie Man – **Muddy Waters**
2. I'd Rather Go Blind – **Etta James**
3. The Thrill Is Gone – **B.B. King**
4. Sunshine of Your Love – **Cream**
5. Smokestack Lightning – **Howlin' Wolf**

B.B. King

The guitar
Guitar notes can be of a similar pitch and sound to singing, which is perfect for the emotional songs in blues music. Like the harmonica, the guitar is also easy to carry.

The 12-bar blues
Blues music often follows a simple form known as the 12-bar blues. This is a 12-bar pattern, repeated for as long as the musician wants.

The basic blues form only has three chords.

A7

D7   A7

E7   D7   A7   A7

1940s Rock and roll starts to evolve from blues music. It generally follows the same 12-bar structure, but with a stronger, faster rhythm.

Rock-and-roll artist Buddy Holly

1966 Jimi Hendrix forms the band The Jimi Hendrix Experience. He experiments with the guitar in blues-style music, adding new electronic effects.

JAZZ

In the early 1900s, in New Orleans, marching band music was adapted by African Americans to create jazz. Jazz musicians often improvise, or make the music up, as they perform. This makes jazz one of the most creative and skillful styles of music.

Roy Haynes

Brushed drums
Jazz drummers often use brushes instead of sticks, in a playing style called brushed drums. The brushes make a soft, sweeping sound as they're dragged back and forth over the snare drum.

Duke Ellington and his band

All together now
Big bands feature multiple brass instruments, such as trumpets and trombones, along with the saxophone. Rhythm sections of such bands include drums, the upright bass, guitar, and the piano.

THE BIG BAND

Big bands became popular in the early 1900s. These large groups of musicians played fast-paced music that was fun to dance to. A swing style, which gives the music a bouncy feel, is common in big band music.

TIMELINE

EARLY 1900s
Jelly Roll Morton, a pianist from New Orleans, becomes one of the earliest jazz musicians.

1920s Duke Ellington records his first music with a big band at the Cotton Club in New York City.

The walking bass line

This style of jazz bassline is played around the notes in the chords of the song. The bassline notes move up or down in a steady, regular pattern, which gives the feel of walking.

Amin 7   D7   Gmin 7   G7

▶ **PLAYLIST**

1. So What – **Miles Davis**
2. Summertime – **Ella Fitzgerald**
3. Cantaloupe Island – **Herbie Hancock**
4. Take 5 – **Dave Brubeck**
5. My Baby Just Cares for Me – **Nina Simone**

Improvisation

Making up music on the spot is called improvisation. Bands often allow each member the chance to improvise a solo. Improvised singing is called scat, for which jazz star Betty Carter was well known.

Betty Carter

The birth of cool

Miles Davis was a jazz trumpet player and composer who helped introduce new styles, such as cool jazz. This has a slower tempo than other types of jazz.

Charlie Mingus

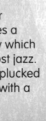

Jazz strings

The upright bass, or double bass, creates a low-pitched melody which can be heard in most jazz. The bass is usually plucked rather than played with a bow in this style .

Miles Davis

1930s Ella Fitzgerald rises to fame. She will later perform to huge crowds in venues around the world.

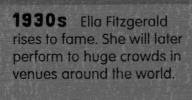

LATE 1930s Virtuoso saxophonist and composer Charlie Parker helps develop bebop, a fast-paced style of jazz.

SEEING MUSIC

Some people don't just hear music, they can see, smell, or even feel it, too. This is called synesthesia, a condition in which a person's senses are joined.

COLORFUL MUSIC

Chromesthesia is a type of synesthesia. People with chromesthesia see colors when they hear sounds. Many famous musicians say they have this, and that it helps them compose music. New Zealand musician Lorde says that she knows when a song is good if it has the right color.

Lorde

Lorde imagines what she wants her song to look like while she composes it.

Each note can appear as a different color.

The sound of an instrument might appear as a certain color.

Senses

Synesthesia blends different senses together. The five main senses are hearing, smell, taste, touch, and sight. These are controlled by separate parts of the brain. Scientists think some types of synesthesia take place when these parts are linked, so two senses are activated at once.

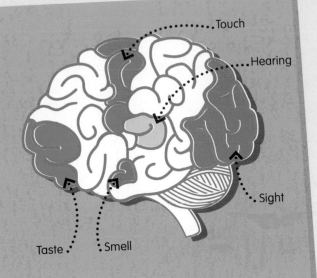

Touch

Hearing

Sight

Taste

Smell

Tasty words

People with lexical-gustatory synesthesia taste foods when they hear unrelated words. A table could be lemon-flavored, or a book might taste like chocolate...

Names can taste like foods, too. Your name might taste like ice cream to some people!

Pressure
It might feel as though something is pressing on an area of skin.

Tingling skin
A sound could cause a tingling sensation, like pins and needles.

TOUCHY-FEELY SOUNDS

Auditory-tactile synesthesia causes people to feel things on their skin when they listen to music or other sounds. It's a little bit like getting goosebumps when you hear a sound, but much stronger!

Bubbles
It could also feel like bubbles are popping on your skin!

MUSICALS

From animated films to spectacular theater shows, musicals feature great stories and catchy music. Live shows are full of eye-catching costumes, slick dancing, storytelling lyrics, and music that builds toward loud and often emotional endings.

GREEK ORIGINS

Musicals began thousands of years ago, in ancient Greece. Music was added to plays—both lighthearted comedies and sad tragedies. The shows were put on in round outdoor theaters, called amphitheaters.

Ancient Greek Theatre of Ephesus

Dream teams
Lyricists create the words that go with a composer's music. Composer Sir Andrew Lloyd Webber and lyricist Tim Rice made many masterpieces, such as *Joseph and the Amazing Technicolor Dreamcoat*.

TIMELINE

C.600s BCE
Theater in ancient Greece combines music with stage shows, using masks to show different characters.

Late 1600s
The Theatre Royal in London, UK, is opened. It is the first theater in the city's famous theater district—the West End.

Sight-reading
Pit musicians must be able to sight-read, which means to play as you read music, rather than remembering it. They can often read music as quickly as we can read words!

▶ PLAYLIST
1. "The Music of the Night" from *The Phantom of the Opera* – **Michael Crawford**
2. "Defying Gravity" from *Wicked* – **Idina Menzel**
3. "I Dreamed a Dream" from *Les Misérables* – **Susan Boyle**
4. "Any Dream Will Do" from *Joseph* – **Jason Donovan**
5. "Memory" from *Cats* – **Elaine Paige**

Jukebox musical
Some artists are so popular that their music is made into a musical—called a jukebox musical. *Mamma Mia* is based on music by the band ABBA. The stage show was made into a hit film.

Triple threats
To star in a musical, you need to sing beautifully, dance flawlessly, and act impressively—making you a triple threat. Vocal exercises help ensure the voice isn't damaged in nightly shows.

Layton Williams scored the main role in *Billy Elliot*, in London's West End, at the age of 12.

Pit musicians
The musicians in a musical theater show usually perform in the pit—a low area in front of the stage. They often play several instruments during the show, called doubling.

Violet Tucker debuted as the lead role in *Matilda*, in the West End, at the age of 10.

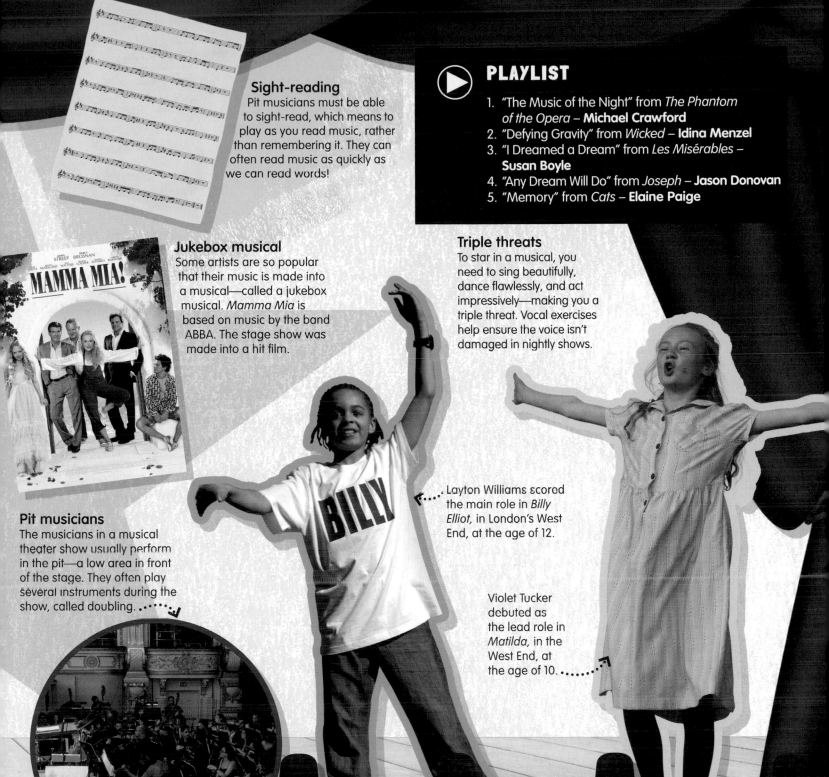

1920s The first films with sound are made. Film companies, called studios, rush to make sound-filled musicals.

The Love Parade

1968 *Joseph and the Amazing Technicolor Dreamcoat* becomes the first show by Sir Andrew Lloyd Webber and Tim Rice to be performed in public.

OPERA

Opera singers have powerful voices that can reach people at the back of theaters. They often vibrate their voice in a technique called vibrato, which helps project, or send out sound. They expertly control their voice to sing complicated music.

Opera star J'Nai Bridges sometimes jogs while training, making it harder to sing, so she can practice control!

THE VOICE

SCAT

This style of singing does not use words. Instead, scat singers make sounds such as "doo," "bah," and "boop." Scat singing is often improvised (made up on the spot), and is commonly used in jazz music.

Ella Fitzgerald sang scat that copied the instruments with which she performed.

Reggie Watts mixes beatboxing and other singing styles to perform on his own.

BEATBOXING

Expert beatboxers use their voice to copy the sounds of an entire drum kit and many other instruments. Some beatboxed tracks sound as though they're made by an entire band.

SCREAMING

Music styles such as metal feature vocalists that scream lyrics. Screaming needs a lot of practice because bad technique can cause a very sore throat, or even lead to long-term voice problems.

George Pettit screamed for the band Alexisonfire, whose music also used a smoother singing style.

To create music, all you need to do is open your mouth and sing. You can make sounds that are high or low, growly or smooth. Listen for these styles of singing in the music you hear every day.

RAP

Rapping is when words are spoken in time to a beat. This can be at a very fast pace, which makes it a tricky skill. Some rappers make up the words as they go along, which is called freestyling.

Rappers such as Stormzy have rap battles—taking turns to make up lines.

SOUL

Soul music features lyrics about emotional topics, such as love. Artists that sing this kind of music often put lots of power into their voice to show strong emotion, in a technique called belting.

Marvin Gaye was a talented soul singer who helped pioneer a soul-inspired genre called Motown.

How do we sing?

When you speak or sing, air is released from your lungs and travels up through the windpipe, or trachea. This makes folds of tissue in the trachea, called the vocal cords, vibrate to create a noise.

You take in and breathe out air through your nose and mouth.

Vocal cords
These are membranes (thin layers of tissue) that sit at the top of your trachea.

Trachea

FUNK

The key ingredient of funk is its groove—that's the tight, rhythmic patterns that get your feet tapping. People love dancing to this uplifting genre, and musicians relish playing it. Since its emergence in the 1960s, funk has influenced many other styles of music.

FUNK'S ORIGINS

In the 1960s, artists such as James Brown started emphasizing the groove in their music. This new music with a cool dance beat became known as funk.

KC and the Sunshine Band
Superstars of the 1970s, this band fused funk and disco in their songs. A brass section, including trumpet and saxophone, added zest and melody to many of their hits.

James Brown
Known as the "Godfather of Soul," singer, songwriter, and dancer James Brown was a pioneer of funk. His band played bold grooves to Brown's inventive lyrics.

TIMELINE

Mid 1960s Funk music develops from songs such as *Papa's Got a Brand New Bag* and *I Got You (I Feel Good)* by James Brown.

1970s George Clinton and his bands Parliament and Funkadelic mix funk, jazz, and psychedelic rock with amazing costumes.

16 strums per bar

In funk music, the guitarist often plays a fast strumming pattern, with 16 strums to a bar. The strings are muted on many of the strums to create a percussive, groovy sound.

▶ PLAYLIST

1. Papa's Got a Brand New Bag – **James Brown**
2. Flash Light – **Parliament**
3. Give It Away – **Red Hot Chilli Peppers**
4. Uptown Funk – **Mark Ronson feat. Bruno Mars**
5. I Feel for You – **Chaka Kahn**

Prince

A songwriter, entertainer, and brilliant guitarist, Prince mixed funk music with other genres, including rock, pop, and soul.

Chic

Funk guitar

The funk guitar adds a rhythmic harmony. It tends to be played with controlled, intricate strumming patterns, or single-note funk lines.

Drum and bass magic

In funk music, the drummer and bass player build the foundations of the groove. These two musicians have a special relationship, and they need to be perfectly in time with each other.

1980s Prince becomes a global superstar, blending funk with other music styles on songs such as *Kiss* and *Sign o' the Times*.

21st century Today, funk is a mainstream genre. Its grooves spice up songs by acts such as Bruno Mars and Daft Punk.

Bruno Mars

ROCK

Rock music is energetic and loud, built around strong bass and drum rhythms. To match their powerful style of music, rock artists often look visually impressive, with flashy clothes or lots of hair. Bands put on fantastic shows, moving wildly to their music.

Freddie Mercury of Queen

ROCK AND ROLL

Rock and roll music, which inspired later rock styles, began in the 1940s. Artists played fast guitar solos and riffs, or repeated snatches of melody, with lots of notes.

The front person
Many rock bands have a singer who is energetic, entertaining, and who wears outfits that stand out. This is the front person. They also have powerful vocals to hit the wide range of notes sung, or shouted, in rock music.

Chuck Berry
Chuck Berry was one of the first rock and roll artists to play electric guitar solos—a key feature of rock.

TIMELINE

1955 Chuck Berry releases his first single, *Maybellene*. It sells more than 1 million copies.

Chuck Berry's guitar

1965 Rock band the Rolling Stones' first single, *Satisfaction,* is released. It will go on to be voted one of the best songs ever by multiple music magazines.

The power chord
Rock features electric-guitar chords played loudly, with lots of distortion, which alters the sound to make it fuzzier. Some tracks use only power chords!

A5   D5   A5   D5

▶ PLAYLIST
1. Don't Stop Me Now – **Queen**
2. Jumpin' Jack Flash – **The Rolling Stones**
3. Sheena Is a Punk Rocker – **The Ramones**
4. Want You Back – **Haim**
5. The Chain – **Fleetwood Mac**

The electric guitar
A symbol of rock, the electric guitar can be made to sound as though it's screaming, to create a long-lasting note at the end of a song, or to play an impressive solo section.

Eric Clapton

Danielle Haim from pop-rock band Haim

The riff
The guitar riff is an important part of rock songs. It acts as a hook—a repeated melody that stays in someone's head after they've heard it.

1970 The band Queen form. They go on to write some of the most popular rock songs in history, winning many awards.

LATE 1970s A style of music called punk erupts from rock music. It features shouty lyrics and fast electric-guitar playing.

Dee Dee Ramone, from punk band The Ramones

WHY DOES MUSIC STICK IN YOUR HEAD?

Music contains features that help you remember it. This is why you might find it easier to recall songs you've heard than words you've read. The problem is, sometimes songs are too memorable and get stuck in your head! Let's find out why.

EMOTION

Music can make you feel strong emotions, like being very happy or very sad. These feelings can make the music much more memorable.

ALLITERATION

Alliteration is the technique of using several words in a row all starting with the same letter. Lyrics that use alliteration are more likely to get stuck in your head.

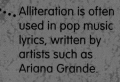

Alliteration is often used in pop music lyrics, written by artists such as Ariana Grande.

Opera characters sing instead of speaking. The songs in operas about sad events can be very emotional.

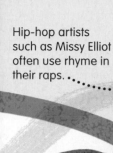

Hip-hop artists such as Missy Elliot often use rhyme in their raps.

PLAYLIST

1. Somebody That I Used to Know – **Gotye**
2. Shape of You – **Ed Sheeran**
3. Happy – **Pharrell Williams**
4. Single Ladies – **Beyoncé**
5. Call Me Maybe – **Carly Rae Jepsen**

RHYME

Words that rhyme (sound similar) are easier to remember than words that don't. Rhyme in old poems and songs that were passed down vocally helped people to remember them.

Learn how rhythm is important in traditional African styles of music on page 17.

RHYTHM

Music has a much stronger rhythm than normal speech. This makes it more memorable, and more likely to stick in your head.

WHAT IS AN EARWORM?

When a song gets stuck in your head it's known as an earworm. Earworms might come to you after listening to a catchy song, or just randomly pop into your head years after hearing a song.

How to throw out an earworm

Tasks that use your brain have been shown to get rid of earworms. These include reading, doing crossword puzzles, or chatting with somebody—maybe not about the earworm, though! It also helps to eat chewy sweets, because using your mouth can get rid of short-term memories.

Rockstar rocks

Pop icon pets

HIP-HOP HATS

RHYTHM

A rhythm is a series of sounds, such as the beats of a drum. The rhythm of a piece helps musicians play at the right speed. They count the beats to follow the same rhythm.

TIME SIGNATURE

Music is made up of small sections, called bars. The time signature tells musicians about the beats in each bar. It's shown as two numbers on a stave: the amount of beats per bar (top), and the type of beat, such as a crotchet (bottom).

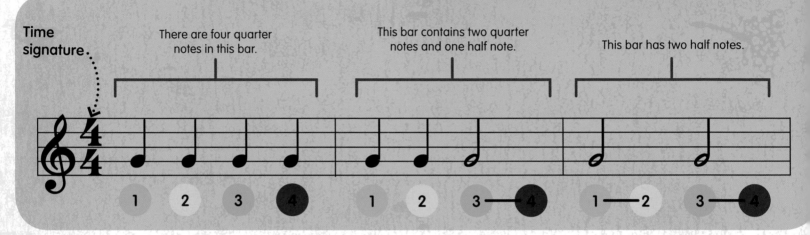

Time signature

There are four quarter notes in this bar.

This bar contains two quarter notes and one half note.

This bar has two half notes.

1　2　3　4　　1　2　3 — 4　　1 — 2　3 — 4

CLAPPING RHYTHMS

A great way to practice rhythms is to clap them. If a note has more than one beat, clap and then hold your hands together for a beat.

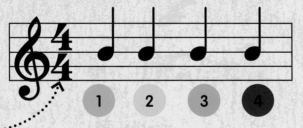

The 4/4 time signature means that there are four beats to a bar, and the quarter note gets the beat.

1　2　3　4

In this time signature, clap four quarter-note beats in each bar.

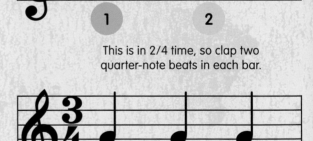

This is in 2/4 time, so clap two quarter-note beats in each bar.

1　2　3

In 3/4 time, clap three quarter-note beats in each bar.

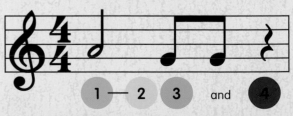

1 — 2　3　and　4

Two eighth notes make up a quarter note, so clap twice for this note, twice as fast as a quarter note. Don't clap on a rest.

TEMPO

Music usually has a speed, which is known as the tempo. The tempo affects how music makes you feel—you might want to nod along, or dance wildly!

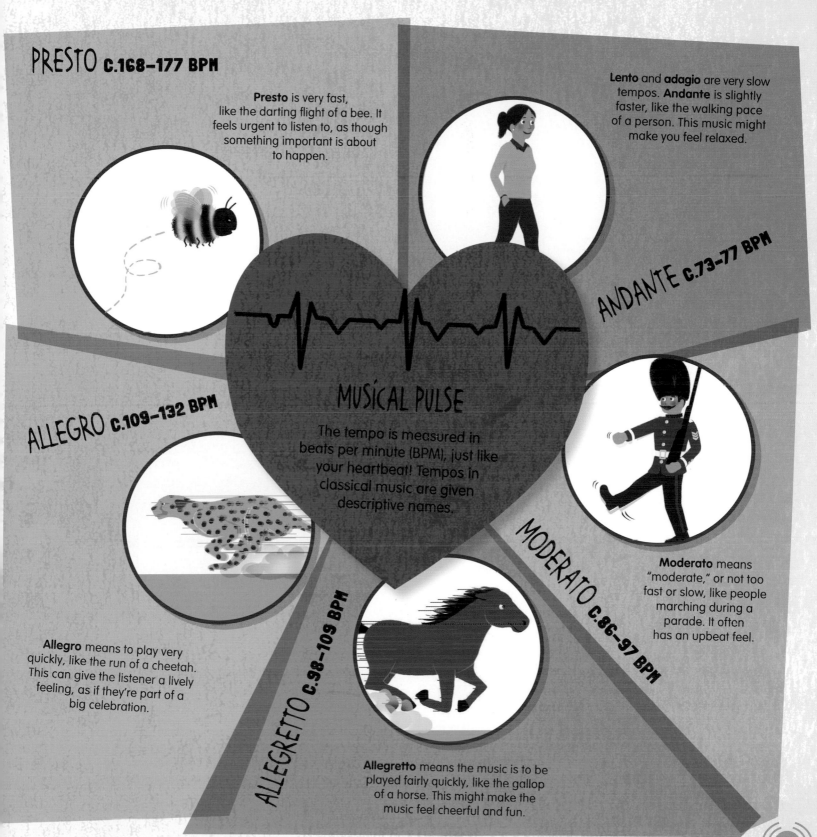

PRESTO c.168–177 BPM

Presto is very fast, like the darting flight of a bee. It feels urgent to listen to, as though something important is about to happen.

Lento and **adagio** are very slow tempos. **Andante** is slightly faster, like the walking pace of a person. This music might make you feel relaxed.

ANDANTE c.73–77 BPM

MUSICAL PULSE

The tempo is measured in beats per minute (BPM), just like your heartbeat! Tempos in classical music are given descriptive names.

ALLEGRO c.109–132 BPM

Allegro means to play very quickly, like the run of a cheetah. This can give the listener a lively feeling, as if they're part of a big celebration.

MODERATO c.86–97 BPM

Moderato means "moderate," or not too fast or slow, like people marching during a parade. It often has an upbeat feel.

ALLEGRETTO c.98–109 BPM

Allegretto means the music is to be played fairly quickly, like the gallop of a horse. This might make the music feel cheerful and fun.

REGGAE

If you're looking for music to play while relaxing in your room, you might want to put on some reggae. Tracks tend to be slower than other music, with distinctive beats. Listen for the influence of reggae in other pop songs, too.

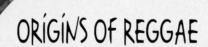

Ska stars Toots and the Maytals

Bob Marley
Jamaica-born Bob Marley began recording in 1962, and later formed a band called Bob Marley and the Wailers. His music is still enjoyed by millions of people today, and he was awarded Jamaica's Order of Merit award.

ORIGINS OF REGGAE

Reggae evolved from ska music in the 1960s. The two genres have a similar feel, with rhythms that stress the second or fourth beat in a bar. However, reggae has a slower tempo and doesn't have ska's brass section.

TIMELINE

1950s Ska begins, combining music styles such as calypso with R&B (rhythm and blues).

The clarinet is popular in both calypso and ska.

MID 1960s Rocksteady emerges—a slower style of ska music, with smaller bands and no brass section.

Desmond Dekker

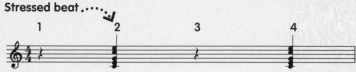
Stressed beat

1   2   3   4

The reggae skank
Reggae features offbeat rhythms, which means every other beat in a bar is stressed. This is also known as the skank. The stressed beat is often played on a guitar or piano, with a short, sharp feel.

Aston Barrett from The Wailers

PLAYLIST
1. No Woman, No Cry – **Bob Marley**
2. Israelites – **Desmond Dekker & The Aces**
3. Young, Gifted and Black – **Bob and Marcia**
4. Monkey Man – **The Maytals**
5. Rapture – **Koffee feat. Govana**

The bass line
The bass plays a catchy, melodic part in reggae, called the bass line. It usually stands out over the guitar and drums in reggae, which play simple, spaced-out chords and beats.

The one drop
The one drop is where the drummer doesn't play, or "drops," the first beat of the bar. This is different from the average rock or pop drumbeat, where the first beat is emphasized.

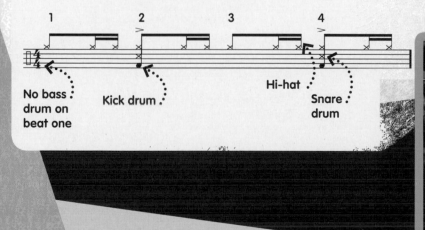

1   2   3   4

No bass drum on beat one

Kick drum

Hi-hat

Snare drum

LATE 1960s Reggae slows the tempo further, creating a more relaxed feel. Artists such as Bob Marley and Lee "Scratch" Perry make the genre popular abroad.

Lee "Scratch" Perry

LATE 1970s Punk rock and ska are blended to form a shoutier ska style—ska punk. No Doubt help make ska punk widely popular in the 1990s.

Gwen Stefani from the band No Doubt

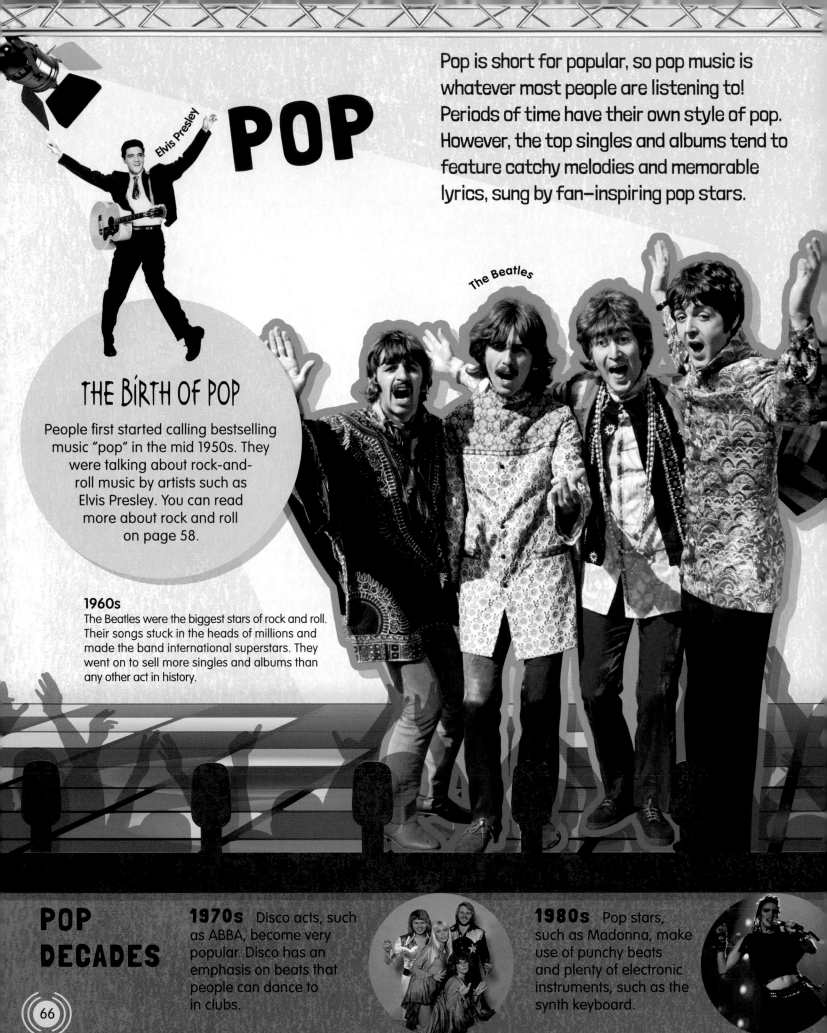

Elvis Presley

POP

Pop is short for popular, so pop music is whatever most people are listening to! Periods of time have their own style of pop. However, the top singles and albums tend to feature catchy melodies and memorable lyrics, sung by fan–inspiring pop stars.

The Beatles

THE BIRTH OF POP

People first started calling bestselling music "pop" in the mid 1950s. They were talking about rock-and-roll music by artists such as Elvis Presley. You can read more about rock and roll on page 58.

1960s
The Beatles were the biggest stars of rock and roll. Their songs stuck in the heads of millions and made the band international superstars. They went on to sell more singles and albums than any other act in history.

POP DECADES

1970s Disco acts, such as ABBA, become very popular. Disco has an emphasis on beats that people can dance to in clubs.

1980s Pop stars, such as Madonna, make use of punchy beats and plenty of electronic instruments, such as the synth keyboard.

The motif

Pop music often makes use of a catchy motif. A motif is a repeating musical phrase or hook that the listener is drawn to.

D   Bmin

I   hope we will   be fine

This motif is from the song *World in Danger* **by Frankie Morland**

Motifs can have accompanying lyrics.

▶ **PLAYLIST**

1. Penny Lane – **The Beatles**
2. Take a Chance on Me – **ABBA**
3. Vogue – **Madonna**
4. Born This Way – **Lady Gaga**
5. Break My Heart – **Dua Lipa**

Lady Gaga

Allessia Cara

Fashion

Pop stars often want to look impressive when they're performing. Many acts wear eye-catching costumes that help create wildly enjoyable live shows.

Vinyl record

Three-minute magic

In the 1920s, songs were recorded on vinyl records, which could only hold around three minutes of music. Artists kept songs to this length, and continue to make songs that are mostly between three to four minutes long today!

Digital age

Allessia Cara started out posting videos of herself singing on YouTube. These were noticed by the founder of a top record label, EP Entertainment.

1990s Britpop acts become popular. They are British rock groups such as Oasis, who are influenced by bands from the 1960s.

2000s Music features lots of elements added digitally, such as electronic beats and samples from other songs or recordings.

Britney Spears

ELECTRIC GUITAR

Unlike acoustic versions, electric string instruments don't need a hollow body to produce their sound. They have flatter, solid bodies with pickups, which pick up the vibrations from the strings.

KEYBOARD

The electric keyboard can mimic several key instruments, such as the piano or the organ. The keys can also be made to play the sounds of other instruments, such as drums.

BASS GUITAR

Like the acoustic (nonelectric) bass, the electric bass has fewer strings and a longer neck than an ordinary guitar. It creates a lower sound, too.

ELECTRIC INSTRUMENTS

ELECTRIC VIOLIN

As with other electric instruments, effects can be added to the violin. These include reverb, which makes a note last longer.

Electricity can zap new life into an instrument by making the sound louder. Notes can be changed using effects to create new, unique sounds. Here are some electric instruments that you can hear in many songs today.

MOOG SYNTHESIZER

This instrument is played using a keyboard, with lots of controls to shape (perfect) the sound. The technique of shaping a sound is called synthesis, which gives the instrument its name.

Pitch antenna
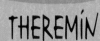

THEREMIN

This unique instrument can be played without touching it at all! The player controls the pitch of a note by moving their hand nearer or farther from the pitch antenna.

VOCODER

This instrument is similar to a synthesizer, but it shapes the sound of a voice. It can transform a singer's beautiful note into a robotic sound, for example.

Digital Audio Workstation (DAW)

This software allows you to create music on your computer. It can be used to put together separately recorded sounds, as well as add virtual instruments, to produce entire tracks.

Amp
An amp (amplifier) produces the electric instrument's sound. It controls the volume, and can add effects.

HOW IT WORKS

Many electric instruments work using an electromagnet, called a pickup. When the instrument's string vibrates, it causes a vibration in the magnetic field and a current in the wire, which is turned into sound by an amplifier.

LOOP PEDAL

This clever device can record an instrument and play it back over and over again, live on stage! It can be used to create complicated music featuring lots of layers.

69

LAYERS OF A SONG

Have you ever wondered how your favorite song began? It might have started with a bit of melody, hummed by the artist. From small beginnings, musicians build layers to make a finished piece.

PADS

These are parts added to fill out the song. Pads can be "oohs" and "aahs" from backing vocalists, or warm synthesizer sounds.

OOOOHHHHH

AAAAHHHHH

Alt J

BACKING VOCALS

As well as padding out a song, additional vocals can support the top line. They can also add vocal harmony, as in Alt J's *Breezeblocks*.

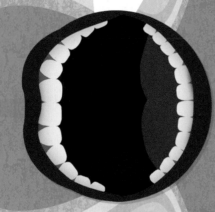

THE TOP LINE

This is the main melody, and can be a catchy hook. The top line is often a lead vocal line which stands out above the other elements.

THE HARMONY

This is the the sound of notes combined as chords, or played on multiple instruments at the same time. Harmony gives the song depth. Harmonious instruments such as the piano and guitar are commonly used to play chords.

OVER AND OVER

In *Shotgun*, George Ezra repeats the vocal top line melody throughout the chorus. Can you hear it?

George Ezra

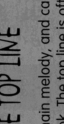

Joe Dart of Vulfpeck

BASS GENIUS

Some bands use bass in an interesting way. In Vulfpeck's *Deantown*, the bass line introduces the melody, while other instruments add harmony. Listen!

THE BASS LINE

This part adds low-pitched bass notes. The bass line works closely with the groove, often matching the beats. It also adds to the harmony.

SOUND EFFECTS

Sound effects can add lots of interest and help capture the listener's imagination. They could be anything, even an animal sound!

THE GROOVE

The foundation of a song is the rhythm, which is also called the groove. It's usually played on the drums, or another percussion instrument. This element will have you nodding or dancing to the music.

INSPIRATION

Anything can inspire a song. You might improvise a cool drum groove, a lovely chord progression, or a melody—or spot something that gives you a lyric idea. Keep a notebook handy for ideas!

▶ **PLAYLIST**

1. Breezeblocks – **Alt J**
2. Shotgun – **George Ezra**
3. Dean Town – **Vulfpeck**
4. Everybody Needs Somebody to Love – **The Rolling Stones** (uses a tambourine to play the groove)
5. Bury a Friend – **Billie Eilish** (uses a scream sound effect)

HIP-HOP

In hip-hop, listen for clever, rapid-fire lyrics, perfectly matched to the beat. As well as skilled wordsmiths, hip-hop musicians are masters of experimentation. They often add beats and rap to existing songs to make brand new music.

THE BRONX

In the 1970s, young African Americans crammed into parties with skilled DJs in the Bronx in New York City. DJs experimented with records, for example by playing some sections for longer, to make hip-hop.

Colorful streets

For many hip-hop fans, graffiti—or street art—is the visual form of hip-hop. Both began as a way for young people in poor places to be creative. Graffiti artists transform the streets, but it's usually illegal!

DJing

Short for "disk jockeying," DJing means to play records for a crowd. Good DJs learn to mix tracks using turntables—splicing together different parts of two records.

Grandmaster Flash

········ Turntable

TIMELINE

EARLY 1970s
DJ Kool Herc starts DJing in the Bronx. He plays with tracks, for example by extending instrumental sections.

1979 The Sugarhill Gang release *Rapper's Delight*—the first rap hit.

Scratching

This technique is when a record is pushed back and forth on a turntable, causing the needle to make a scratching sound. DJs use this effect creatively to make catchy rhythms.

Sampling

A sample is a section of music from another song, or a whole song, which is used in a new piece. Hip-hop artists often change the sample's pitch or tempo, or loop a section so it plays on repeat, to make it their own.

Rapping

Rappers follow the beat of a track by stressing certain words, and often use rhymes to help the rap flow. Rapping began with MCs (masters of ceremony) introducing and then talking over the music played by DJs at early hip-hop parties.

Jay Z

Breakdancing

Hip-hop has its own energetic dance style—breakdancing. It features moves that use the whole body, like gymnastics. It gets its name from a drum section in songs called "the break."

1984 Def Jam Records is launched. It becomes an important record label for hip-hop artists.

Def Jam artist Kanye West

2008 Jay-Z is the first hip-hop artist to headline (appear as the star performer) at Glastonbury Festival's Pyramid stage.

WHY DO WE MOVE TO MUSIC?

People can be found dancing all around the world. Why is it that we tap our feet, nod our heads, and clap our hands to music? Scientists have lots of ideas!

BRAIN CONNECTIONS

Scientists studied which areas of the brain were made active when people listened to music. They found that music triggers the areas of the brain linked with movement.

Supplementary motor area

Primary motor cortex

Premotor cortex

Cerebellum

········ Happy chemicals released when we dance include endorphins and serotonin.

FEEL-GOOD STUFF

Both music and dancing cause our bodies to release chemicals that make us feel good. We're more likely to do things that make us feel good, so we dance to music for double the chemicals!

Dancing can make us better at dealing with pain!

KEEPING THE BEAT

We may be born with a love of dance! Most babies respond to music by moving to the beat. We carry this impulse to dance into adulthood, as well as our ability to spot tempo.

Babies move their arms, heads, and legs to the beat.

Groups of dancers are called troupes.

EVOLUTIONARY

To do group tasks such as hunting, early humans needed to work in sync—which means together. We may enjoy dancing because it helps us learn to stay in sync with one another, as we follow a beat.

It took a group of humans to hunt a woolly mammoth.

SOCIAL

Being in sync doesn't just help us do practical tasks, it also makes us feel connected to one another. People love making friends, so we enjoy dancing with others!

AROUND THE WORLD

Music can be inspired by religion, politics, art, or even the weather, which might explain why different styles spring up from country to country. Let's take a look at some popular styles from around the world.

RHYTHM AND BLUES

Rhythm and blues, or R&B, developed from blues music in the US. It is a livelier style with a heavier groove.

IRISH FOLK

Upbeat folk music from Ireland features guitars, fiddles, whistles, and various percussion instruments.

SKA

This fast-paced, danceable genre began in Jamaica in the mid-1900s. Reggae and rocksteady are styles that evolved from ska.

SALSA

Cuba's best-known type of music uses regular beats for couples to dance to. It features lots of rhythmic percussion.

CUMBIA

From Colombia, Cumbia is a percussive style of music. It has an accompanying type of dance that uses simple steps to fit the beat.

BRITPOP

This style of pop-rock from the 1990s was influenced by 1960s rock. However, it was a softer sound and easier to sing along to.

RUSSIAN FOLK

Traditional Russian music features beautiful vocal melodies and harmonies, and, often, the balalaika.

CANTOPOP

Chinese cantopop features an uplifting pop structure with singing in Cantonese—one of the languages from China.

FLAMENCO

This Spanish genre has a dramatic accompanying dance, with foot stomping to match the beat. It often uses castanets and guitars.

CITY POP

A polished, upbeat genre, Japan's city pop is heavily influenced by pop music from the US and Europe.

LAÏKÓ

Greek pop music inspired by the country's traditional styles, such as folk, is called Laïkó—which means "popular music."

BALADI

This traditional Egyptian style often accompanies belly dancing. It tends to features a pair of hand drums called a tabla.

BOLLYWOOD

This music is written for India's Bollywood films. It fuses Indian classical music with US genres, such as R&B and hip hop.

GAMELAN

This Indonesian style is relaxing to listen to. It is played by an ensemble, and features lots of melodic and rhythmic repetition.

MBUBE

In this South African style, groups sing a capella (without backing instruments). It features beautiful harmonics.

AFROBEAT

This lively genre of dance music from Nigeria fuses traditional African music with funk and jazz.

K-POP

All-singing, all-dancing K-pop emerged in South Korea—which is what the "K" stands for. This polished, electronic pop features drum-machine beats and is sung by groups of stars, called idols, who have huge worldwide followings.

Arms folded

Star jump

iDOL ORiGiNS

The first K-pop idol group was put together by a record producer in 1996, after he asked school students to describe their perfect pop group. Now, people audition for K-pop groups and spend lots of time training to sing and dance like pros.

Auditions this way →

Dance

K-pop artists aren't just masterful music makers, they're also amazing dancers. K-pop groups spend hours a day practicing dances for show-stopping music videos and live performances.

Crouch

BTS

TIMELINE

1992 Hip-hop group Seo Taiji & Boys release their first album, making South Korean hip-hop popular for the first time.

Seo Taiji

1995 Talent agency and record label SM Entertainment launches, with the aim of creating pop groups. H.O.T. and S.E.S. are early successes.

Choi Sung-hee

Girls' Generation

PLAYLIST
1. Blood Sweat & Tears – **BTS**
2. Gee – **Girls' Generation**
3. Ko Ko Bop – **EXO**
4. TT – **Twice**
5. Kill This Love – **Blackpink**

Visual impact
K-pop groups spend time and effort perfecting their image. They might wear outfits tied together by a color, in a similar style. Music videos make use of beautiful costumes and impressive sets.

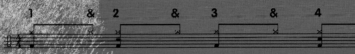

Drum beat
K-pop music is generally in 4/4 time, with a heavy beat on each beat of the bar. This is know as "4 to the floor," and is also commonly found in electronic dance music.

HELLO

Two languages
K-pop songs often use a mixture of Korean and English, so that people in countries outside of South Korea understand the words and sing along.

안녕하세요

Mixing styles
K-pop puts together elements from many genres. You might spot the drum-machine beats of electronic dance music and hip-hop rapping in the same track.

Hip-hop star Alicia Keys

EDM artist Avicii

2012 PSY's *Gangman Style* becomes a global hit and the first YouTube video to reach a billion views. People begin to take notice of K-pop worldwide.

2018–2019 BTS become the first K-pop band to top the U.S album chart, and release three number-one albums in the space of a year.

BEHIND THE SCENES

Most of the music you listen to isn't just made by the artist. A whole team of musicians help to make it happen. Let's take a look at some of the important roles in the music industry.

THE ARTIST

The artist writes songs and makes basic recordings, called demos—short for demonstrations.

MANAGER

The manager has lots of connections and knows the music business very well. They can help an artist plan their journey from demos to released songs.

RECORD LABEL

The record label pays for the music to be recorded. This includes hiring the recording studios and promoting the music, which means making lots of people aware of it.

SONGWRITER

Some artists write alone, but working with a songwriter can help to perfect an early demo, or to write completely new songs!

RECORD PRODUCER

The producer knows how to make a song sound great and might have creative musical ideas that really make your song stand out.

SESSION MUSICIAN

Artists hire session musicians to record the instrumental parts of their music and for live performances.

Tour promoter

The promoter organizes venues, ticket prices, and more, to get the show on the road!

THE MUSIC BECOMES A RECORD

PROMOTION AND TOUR

The artist does interviews online, in magazines, and on television, and uses social media, such as Instagram, to get the music out there. Next up is a showstopping tour to perform the record!

Sound engineer

The music sounds clear and loud enough when it's performed on stage thanks to sound engineers.

···· Lighting rig

Lighting engineer

Dazzling light shows are put on by lighting engineers to make the tour as awesome as possible.

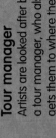

Tour manager

Artists are looked after by a tour manager, who also gets them to where they need to be on time.

ELECTRONIC MUSIC

Electronic music uses sounds created electronically, either by instruments, such as synthesizers, or computers. You might hear tuneful bleeps, voices with strange effects added, or a fast drumbeat that would be very hard for a human to reproduce!

EDM

Electronic dance music (EDM) is one of the most popular styles of electronic music. It features fast electronic beats for energetic dancing, often with a heavy thumping sound.

Fast drumming

The Roland 808 is a popular drum machine, which creates drum beats of different tempos and pitches. It was released in the 1980s as one of the first drum machines to allow people to create their own rhythms.

Deadmau5

TIMELINE

1920 Leon Theremin invents the theremin—an early electronic instrument. Learn more on page 69.

1965 The moog synthesizer becomes the first synthesizer to be sold in stores.

Benoît and the Mandelbrots

Live-coding

Computer code is a set of instructions for a computer to follow. Lines of code can trigger different rhythms or instruments to create music. Some clever musicians improvise tracks live, using code.

Synth magic

Synthesizers are electrical instruments that can be used to create unique sounds. The note can be adjusted in different ways to achieve the right sound.

Attack is how the note begins, either coming in quickly or gently building in volume.

A

D

Decay is how quickly the note drops from its full volume to the sustain volume.

S

R

Release is how the note ends after the musician stops playing, whether instantly or gradually fading out.

Sustain is the note's volume after the decay.

DAWs

Anyone can create electronic music using a DAW (Digital Audio Workstation). There are thousands of sounds to choose from and build into a punchy track. To learn more about DAWs turn to page 69.

1969 An electronic track called *Popcorn* is released by Gershon Kingsley. It is often described as the first EDM track.

1977 The first DAW is released. It replaces tape machines as the most popular way to record music.

IN THE STUDIO

Musicians often sound different when they play live than they do on recorded tracks. This is because they record their music in a studio, which is full of knobs and dials that control how the music sounds. Most studios are run by a producer, who records the music and puts the tracks together.

Home recording

Many people make great quality recordings at home, using computers with digital audio workstation (DAW) software, which can be used to make music, and a sound card. The card is plugged into the computer, to convert sounds into digital signals that can be adjusted.

KNOW YOUR STUDIO

1 **Monitor speaker volume** allows the producer to change the loudness of the sounds coming from the live room.

2 **Monitor screens** with digital audio workstation (DAW) controls, which show picture versions of the sounds coming from each instrument. The images help the producer adjust the music.

3 **Live room** in which the musicians record, with soundproof walls to block outside noise.

4 **Monitor speaker** allows the producer to hear the instruments, so they can let the musicians know if something doesn't sound right.

5 **Level meters** allow the producer to make sure each instrument is loud enough on the recording.

6 **Mute and solo buttons** for the channels that carry sound from each instrument. The buttons allow the sounds to be muted (silenced) or made solo (the only sound).

7 **Scribble strip** to name each channel, so the producer knows which instrument or voice is on each channel.

8 **Transport controls** allow the producer to begin recording, or to play back the music, including stopping, rewinding, or forwarding it.

GAME CHANGERS

Music stars are always experimenting with different styles—that's how music changes over time. These are just a few of the musicians that have helped develop types of music, or even invent new styles, throughout history.

WOLFGANG AMADEUS MOZART (1756-1791)

Born in Austria, Wolfgang had begun writing music by the age of five. He composed more than 600 classical works, including operas. Wolfgang perfected existing forms, such as the opera comique's ensemble finale, in which characters sing different things at once. Wolfgang made this part longer and more complex.

ANTONÍN DVOŘÁK (1841-1904)

A Czech musician, Antonin was already a talented violin player by the age of six. During his career, Antonin composed symphonies, chamber music, operas, and more, developing unique composition styles. He combined elements from German symphonies with those of Bohemian folk and, later, African American music.

JOHN LEE HOOKER (1917-2001)

American guitarist and songwriter John Lee Hooker created his own style of blues music by using the electric guitar and distinct rhythms. His music was also some of the first to include elements of talking blues, a music style using spoken word.

BEBE & LOUIS BARRON
(1925-2008 / 1920-1989)

Bebe and Louis were a musically gifted husband-and-wife team from the US. They were some of the first musicians to compose electronic music, and put it on tape—a recording device. They also composed the first electronic film score.

DAVID BOWIE
(1947-2016)

An English singer-songwriter, David Bowie was an artist who pushed the boundaries of music, fashion, and performance. He experimented with rock and electronic elements to create pop music, and sold more than 100 million albums.

BJÖRK
(1965-now)

Bjork is an experimental pop artist from Iceland, whose music combines elements from many different genres, such as classical and electronica. Her unique voice and exciting mix of genres creates a distinctive sound.

STEP ONE

Participants were put into three different groups. For ten minutes, one group listened to a piece of music by Mozart, one sat in silence, and the final group listened to instructions to relax.

One group were played Mozart's *Sonata for Two Pianos in D Major*.

THE MOZART EFFECT

In 1993 scientists conducted an experiment to discover whether music really does make you more intelligent. They played music by Wolfgang Amadeus Mozart to some students before giving them a test.

STEP TWO

Each group completed the same test. The experiment was redone using multiple tests, with one measuring how well participants could match unfolded and folded shapes.

STEP THREE

Scientists looked at the tests done by each group to see how well they did. If music makes people smarter, then the group that listened to Mozart should have done better...

On the paper-shapes test, the groups that didn't listen to Mozart got more questions wrong.

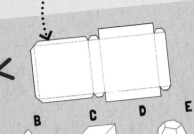

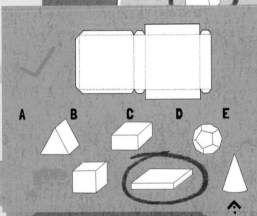

HOW iT WORKS

It's not just Mozart that improves your brain. Other experiments have found that different music also increases brain power. Scientists think this is because your brain is active when listening to music, so it's alert and ready for a test.

The group that listened to Mozart were more likely to get the correct paper-shapes answers—though the effect only lasted for 15 minutes.

Rats

In another experiment, rats were played Mozart while still inside their mothers' stomachs. They were better at completing mazes than rats that weren't played Mozart!

Long-term effects

Scientists have found that children who learn instruments do better at other subjects in school, such as science and English.

Fungi are neither plants nor animals.

MUSIC THROUGH TIME

You can trace back the use of music for many thousands of years. There are some fascinating developments along the way! Let's take a look at some of the key moments in the history of music.

The first percussion
Prehistoric instruments were rocks banged together to make percussive sounds. People had probably been singing for a long time before this point.

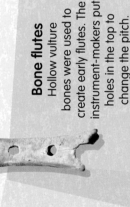

John Dunstable
Working in the 1400s, this composer created some of the first music with major and minor harmony.

c.60,000– 30,000 BCE

Bone flutes
Hollow vulture bones were used to create early flutes. The instrument-makers put holes in the top to change the pitch.

c.38,000 BCE

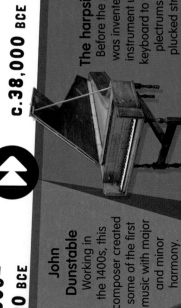

The harpsichord
Before the piano was invented, this instrument used a keyboard to control plectrums that plucked strings.

1300s

Canon in D
Johann Pachelbel wrote one of the most famous pieces of classical music, featuring a canon structure.

1400s

Musical bow
Historians think ancient people may have made music by plucking the strings of their hunting bows.

c.13,000 BCE

Modern music system
Guido d'Arezzo developed a system of writing music. It evolved into the one used today.

1000s

Johann Sebastian Bach
This well-known baroque composer was born in Germany.

Shell trumpets
Conch shells were used as early trumpets. Players pursed their lips to create a sound as they blew through the hollow shell.

c.17,000– 12,000 BCE

Written music
A melody was engraved onto a clay tablet, in modern-day Syria. It is called the Hurrian Hymn and is the first known written piece of music.

c.1400s BCE

The piano
Bartolomeo Cristofori invented the piano in Italy.

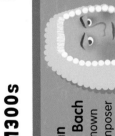

c.1700

Wolfgang Amadeus Mozart
This famous musician was born in Austria. He began writing his own music by the age of six.

1756

1680

168

1700

Ludwig van Beethoven
This German composer was born. With his work, a new age of classical music began—the Romantic era.

1770

The phonograph
Thomas Edison invented the first machine that could record and play back sound. It etched lines onto a cylinder to record, and ran a stylus over the lines to recreate the vibrations.

1877

The gramophone
Emile Berliner invented an improved device for recording and playing back sound. It was the first to record onto disks, called records.

1887

Duke Ellington
This famous jazz composer was born. He created his first music by ear, rather than writing it down.

1899

Jazz
A new form of music began, based on earlier styles such as blues.

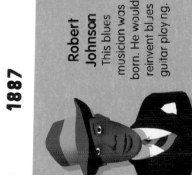

Robert Johnson
This blues musician was born. He would reinvent blues guitar playing.

1911

EARLY 1900s

Modern tape machines
A new way to record music was invented, using magnetic tape. The music was recorded as lines onto the tape, to be played back in machines.

1934

The electric guitar
The first electric guitar was invented by George Beauchamp. It was known as "the frying pan" because of its shape.

1932

The Beatles
The most well-known band in history was formed in Liverpool, England. Their music would inspire generations of music artists to come.

1957

The Moog Synthesizer
Robert Moog released the invention that revolutionized modern music.

1964

Music festivals
Modern music festivals, such as Woodstock, began. They drew huge crowds.

1960s

Glastonbury
The most famous festival in the world today was first put on in Somerset, England. More than 200,000 people flock to the site each year.

1970

DAWs
Creating music was made easier with the invention of the Digital Audio Workstation, or DAW.

1978

CDs
Using new technology, music could be recorded digitally to compact disks (CDs). They were the main format for playing music for many years.

1982

Napster 2.0
Created in this year, Napster 2.0 was the first streaming service that charged users a monthly fee to listen to tracks from a digital music library.

2003

Spotify
The most popular music streaming service today was released in this year. Artists are paid a small amount of money every time someone listens to one of their songs.

2006

GLOSSARY

It's helpful to know these words when learning or talking about music.

amplification
When a sound is made louder, typically by using an electronic amplifier

call and response
Vocal music in which a singer's call is answered by a chorus's response

canon
When the same melody is layered during a piece, with different starting points

chord progression
Sequence of chords played one after the other

composer
Somebody who writes music

digital audio workstation (DAW)
Electronic device for recording, putting together, and editing music

fugue
Piece based around a main melody (the subject) that is repeated and changed throughout, for example by speeding it up or slowing it down

groove
Rhythmic feel to a piece of music

half step
Small interval, also known as a semitone—on a piano, this is one note to the next note.

harmony
Two or more notes played at the same time

hook
Catchy part of a song which the listener often remembers

improvisation
Creating music on the spot, either alone or accompanied by other musicians

interval
Distance between two notes

key
Set of notes, shown with a key signature when written down

lyricist
Somebody who writes song lyrics or poetry

major
Type of harmony with a major third interval, often defined as having a happy sound

minor
Type of harmony with a minor third interval, often defined as having a sad sound

motif
Short musical phrase, which is often added to or otherwise changed during a piece

octave
Distance from one note to the same note in the next highest or lowest register

pitch
Highness or lowness of a note

record label
Business that helps musicians create and sell music

riff
Musical phrase which tends to be a memorable part of a song, and is often repeated throughout the piece

sample
Section of music taken from an existing song or another sound used in a new piece of music

scale
Set sequence of notes

score
All the parts of a song or composition written as sheet music

sheet music
Music written down for musicians to play

singer-songwriter
Somebody who can sing, play, and write music

social media
Online platforms where people can communicate and share ideas

solo
Section of music in which an instrument is performed on its own, or a singer performs vocally on their own, sometimes with accompanying instruments

stress
Emphasis placed on a beat

tempo
Speed at which music is played, measured in BPM (beats per minute)

track
Another name for a recorded song

upbeat
Music played with a joyful feel, often (but not always) with a quicker tempo

virtuoso
Somebody who has achieved a very high level of technical musical ability, for example as an instrumentalist

vocal
Something spoken or sung

whole step
An interval, also known as a tone—on a piano this is two notes or two half steps

MARKINGS

Music has its own language of markings. Learn about some of the most common ones here!

accent
Small pointer above a note, which means to accent a note (play it louder)

fermata
Symbol above a note meaning to pause for longer than the value of the note, or until a conductor indicates

rall.

rallentando
Writing above stave, which means to gradually slow down

 = 120

tempo
Note and number showing the tempo in BPM (beats per minute)

bass clef
Symbol at the beginning of a staff, showing the order of notes on the staff for instruments with a lower pitch (also called the F clef)

flat accidental
Symbol next to a note, which means to flatten it (makes it lower in pitch) by a half step

repeat dots
These dots can be placed at the beginning and end of a section which repeats; it saves writing the passage of music multiple times

ties
Curved line between notes of the same pitch, indicating that the note should last for the length of both note values

A7

chords
A letter or a letter and a number are often used to show a specific chord

glissando
Symbol above notes, showing that players should slide or glide between notes

rhythm clef
This clef is used to indicate nonpitched percussive sounds, such as those on a drum kit; it is also known as the neutral clef

treble clef
Symbol at the beginning of a staff, showing the order of notes on the staff for instruments with a higher pitch (also called the G clef)

crescendo
Symbol below a staff showing that the music gets louder

ledger lines
Lines added to notes written above and below the staff, to show which notes they are

sharp accidental
Symbol next to a note, which means to sharpen it (makes it higher in pitch) by a half step

diminuendo
Symbol below a staff showing that the music gets quieter

natural accidental
Symbol next to a sharpened or flattened note that brings it back to its normal pitch

staccato
Dot under or above a note to show that it should be played shortly and sharply

INDEX

ACKNOWLEDGMENTS

The publisher would like to thank Helen Peters for the index and the following for their kind permission to reproduce their photographs:

(Key: a-above; b-below/bottom; c-center; f-far; l-left; r-right; t-top)

1 Dorling Kindersley: National Music Museum (tl/Harp). Dreamstime.com: Alison Gibson (tl, b, tr). iStockphoto.com: Quirky Mundo (c). iStockphoto.com: Quirky Mundo (c). 2 iStockphoto.com: Quirky Mundo (crb). 2–3 Dreamstime.com: Alison Gibson (Background). 4 Dreamstime.com: Alison Gibson (bl, t); Ba-mi (cla). iStockphoto.com: Quirky Mundo (fbl). 4–5 Dreamstime.com: Alison Gibson (bc, t). iStockphoto.com: Quirky Mundo (c). 5 Dreamstime.com: Alison Gibson (br). iStockphoto.com: Quirky Mundo (tr). 6–7 iStockphoto.com: Quirky Mundo. 6 Alamy Stock Photo: MediaPunch Inc (crb). Dreamstime.com: Alison Gibson (c). 7 Alamy Stock Photo: Everett Collection Inc (tc). Dreamstime.com: Alison Gibson (cr). Rex by Shutterstock: Frank Micelotta / PictureGroup (br). 8 Dreamstime.com: Lars Christensen / C-foto (cb). 8–9 iStockphoto.com: Quirky Mundo. 9 Dreamstime.com: Frenc (crb); Yifang Zhao (c, cr); Alison Gibson (br). 12–13 Dreamstime.com: Alison Gibson (Texture). 12 iStockphoto.com: Quirky Mundo (ca). 14–15 iStockphoto.com: MediaProduction (cl, br); Ryan Pike (bl). 14 Dreamstime.com: Alison Gibson (cl, br); Ryan Pike (bl). 15 Dreamstime.com: Alison Gibson (bl, br, cr, tl). iStockphoto.com: es_sooyon (tr). 16 Dorling Kindersley: Powell-Cotton Museum, Kent (cl). Dreamstime.com: Dmitry Pichugin (bc). 16–17 Alamy Stock Photo: MusicLive. iStockphoto.com: Hudiemm (cb); Quirky Mundo (t). 17 123RF: svrid79 (bc). Alamy Stock Photo: Robert Burch (cra); ZUMA Press, Inc. (c); North Wind Picture Archives (cr). Dreamstime.com: Alison Gibson (tl, tc). 20–21 Dreamstime.com: Alison Gibson. 20 Alamy Stock Photo: Michael Brito (cb). Dreamstime.com: Alison Gibson (crb). Rex by Shutterstock: Richard Young (clb). 21 Dreamstime.com: Alison Gibson (clb, cra). Getty Images: Jo Hale (cb); Hulton Archive (crb). 22–23 Dreamstime.com: Alison Gibson (cb). iStockphoto.com: Quirky Mundo (b). 22 Alamy Stock Photo: Lebrecht Music & Arts (br/Antonio Vivaldi). Dorling Kindersley: National Music Museum (b). Dreamstime.com: Alison Gibson (br). iStockphoto.com: Quirky Mundo (cl, tr). 23 Alamy Stock Photo: GL Archive (br). Dorling Kindersley: National Music Museum (bc). Getty Images: Hiroyuki Ito (tl, crb). 24–25 Dreamstime.com: Alison Gibson (c, cb, b). iStockphoto.com: RedKoalaDesign (t). 24 Alamy Stock Photo: Arunabh Bhattacharjee (cb); Chronicle of World History (br). Dreamstime.com: 7xpert (bc). iStockphoto.com: Quirky Mundo (c). 25 Dreamstime.com: Worldshots (c). Getty Images: Raj K Raj / Hindustan Times (br); Jack Vartoogian (cr). Rex by Shutterstock: AP (bc). 26–27 Dreamstime.com: Alison Gibson. 26 Alamy Stock Photo: GL Archive (c); Lebrecht Music & Arts (cll); World History Archive (cr). 27 Alamy Stock Photo: ITAR–TASS News Agency (cla); Pictorial Press Ltd (ca); Keystone Press (cra). 28–29 Dreamstime.com: Alison Gibson (b). 28 Dreamstime.com: Alison Gibson (l, clb). iStockphoto.com: Quirky Mundo (cl). 29 Dreamstime.com: Alison Gibson (cr, t); Yifang Zhao (clb). 30–31 iStockphoto.com: Quirky Mundo. 30 Dorling Kindersley: Stephen Oliver (cb). 32–33 Dreamstime.com: Alison Gibson (cb, c, b). iStockphoto.com: Quirky Mundo (t). 32 Alamy Stock Photo: Alfredo Garcia Saz (cr). Getty Images: DEA Picture Library / De Agostini (bc); Paul Marotta (l). The Metropolitan Museum of Art, New York: Gift of Mrs. Francis L. Noble, 1935 (tr). 33 Alamy Stock Photo: DPA Picture Alliance (cb); Albert Knapp (clb); Lebrecht Music & Arts (br); ITAR–TASS News Agency (cra). Getty Images: Robbie Jack / Corbis (bc). Rex by Shutterstock: Alastair Muir (c). 34–35 iStockphoto.com: Quirky Mundo. 34–55 Dreamstime.com: Alison Gibson. 36–37 Dreamstime.com: Alison Gibson (t, cb, b). 36 Alamy Stock Photo: INTERFOTO (br). Dreamstime.com: Andreykuzmin (cl/Sign). Getty Images: CBS (cr). iStockphoto.com: Quirky Mundo (cl). Mary Evans Picture Library: (bc). 37 Alamy Stock Photo: Richard Etteridge (tll); imageBROKER (c); Mark Reinstein (bc); Dean Fardell / Alamy Live News Feed (br). 38 123RF.com: Gresei (tr/Violin). Dreamstime.com: Alison Gibson (t, b, tr). 38–39 Dreamstime.com: Alison Gibson (bc). 39 Alamy Stock Photo: Historic Images (br/Aeolian harp). Dorling Kindersley: National Music Museum (c); Royal Academy of Music (tr/Guitar). Dreamstime.com: Alison Gibson (tl, tr, cr, cb, br). iStockphoto.com: Denyshutter (ca); Quirky Mundo (t). 40–41 Dreamstime.com: Alison Gibson (cb, t/Background, b). iStockphoto.com: MaksymChechel (t). 40 Alamy Stock Photo: ClassicStock (cla); The Picture Art Collection (bc). Getty Images: GAB Archive / Redferns (br); Shirlaine Forrest / WireImage (c). iStockphoto.com: Quirky Mundo (cl). 41 Alamy Stock Photo: Gonzales Photo (cla); Charlie Raven (cr); Photo 12 (bc). Getty Images: Steve Larson / The Denver Post (cra); Jason Squires / WireImage (br). iStockphoto.com: Quirky Mundo (t). 42–43 Dreamstime.com: Alison Gibson. 42 Alamy Stock Photo: The Picture Art Collection (clb). 44–45 Dreamstime.com: Alison Gibson (ca). 44 Dreamstime.com: Alison Gibson (bl, c, crb). 45 Dreamstime.com: Alison Gibson (c, cb). iStockphoto.com: Kickstand (bl); Quirky Mundo (crb). 46–47 Dreamstime.com: Alison Gibson (t, cb, b). 46 Alamy Stock Photo: From Original Negative (cra); Pictorial Press Ltd (bc); Heritage Image Partnership Ltd (bc). Dreamstime.com: Thomas Söllner (tc). Getty Images: The Print Collector / Print Collector (cl). iStockphoto.com: Slobo (br). 47 Alamy Stock Photo: Historic Collection (bc). Getty Images: Michael Ochs Archives (cla, cr). Rex by Shutterstock: Marc Sharratt (br). 48–49 Dreamstime.com: Alison Gibson (t, cb, b). 48 Alamy Stock Photo: Pictorial Press Ltd (br); Science History Images (bc). Dreamstime.com: Thomas Söllner (tc). Getty Images: National Jazz Archive / Heritage Images (ca); Transcendental Graphics (cl). iStockphoto.com: Quirky Mundo (crb). 49 Alamy Stock Photo: AF archive (cla); Pictorial Press Ltd (bc). Dreamstime.com: Thomas Söllner (tc). Getty Images: James Kriegsmann / Michael Ochs Archives (br); David Redfern / Redferns (bc). Rex by Shutterstock: Kyle Gustafson / For The Washington Post (cr). iStockphoto.com: MediaProduction (br). 50 Getty Images: Kyle Gustafson / For The Washington Post (cr). iStockphoto.com: MediaProduction (br). 50–51 Dreamstime.com: Alison Gibson. iStockphoto.com: Quirky Mundo (c). 52–53 Dreamstime.com: Alison Gibson (t, cb, b). iStockphoto.com: Quirky Mundo (c). 52 Alamy Stock Photo: Granger Historical Picture Archive (br); WENN Rights Ltd (cr). Dreamstime.com: Igor Zubkov (bc/Theatre Masks). iStockphoto.com: Quirky Mundo (c, bc). Pixabay: 12019 (clb). 53 Alamy Stock Photo: Allstar Picture Library Limited (cla); Nick Savage (cr); B.O'Kane (clb); Glasshouse Images (bc). Getty Images: GAB Archive / Redferns (br); SAV / FilmMagic (c). 54 Alamy Stock Photo: EFE News Agency (ca); Keystone Press (c); Everett Collection Inc (cb). Dreamstime.com: Alison Gibson (tl, cl, bl). 54–55 Alamy Stock Photo: Lebrecht Music & Arts (bc). Dreamstime.com: Alison Gibson (tc). 55 Alamy Stock Photo: Gary Mather (ca). Dreamstime.com: Alison Gibson (crb, tr). iStockphoto.com: Quirky Mundo (cr, br). Rex by Shutterstock: Globe Photos / Mediapunch (c). 56–57 Dreamstime.com: Alison Gibson (t, cb, b). iStockphoto.com: Wi6995 (cb/Rainbow colors). 56 Alamy Stock Photo: Pictorial Press Ltd (bc). Dreamstime.com: Thomas Söllner (tl). Getty Images: (cr); Dimitrios Kambouris / WireImage (c); Photo by Echoes / Redferns (br). iStockphoto.com: Quirky Mundo (cla). 57 Alamy Stock Photo: ZUMA Press Inc (br). Dreamstime.com: Thomas Söllner (tr). Getty Images: Bertrand Guay / AFP (cl); James Andanson / Sygma (cra); Richard E. Aaron / Redferns (bc). 58–59 Dreamstime.com: Alison Gibson (t, cb, b); Thomas Söllner (t/Light). Getty Images: Denis O'Regan (c). iStockphoto.com: PhatsaYui (cb/Stripe). 58 Alamy Stock Photo: Tim Brown (bc). Getty Images: Matthew Baker (br); Michael Ochs Archives (cl). iStockphoto.com: Quirky Mundo (c, ca). 59 Alamy Stock Photo: Christian Bertrand (c); Gijsbert Hanekroot (cla). Getty Images: Michael Putland (br); Ebet Roberts / Redferns (bc). 60 Getty Images: Kevin Mazur / Getty Images for AG (br); Jack Vartoogian (bl). 60–61 iStockphoto.com: Quirky Mundo (c). 61 Alamy Stock Photo: B Christopher (cr). Getty Images: Kevin Mazur / WireImage (t). iStockphoto.com: Gannet77 (br). 62–63 iStockphoto.com: Quirky Mundo. 64–65 Dreamstime.com: Alison Gibson (t, cb, b). iStockphoto.com: Alabady (cb/Jamaica flag). 64 Alamy Stock Photo: John Bentley (br). Getty Images: Michael Ochs Archives (cl); Gijsbert Hanekroot / Redferns (cr). iStockphoto.com: Quirky Mundo (cb). 65 Alamy Stock Photo: Concert Photos (br). Getty Images: C Brandon / Redferns (cr); Ollie Millington / Redferns (bc). 66–67 Dreamstime.com: Alison Gibson (t, cb, b); Thomas Söllner (t/Light). iStockphoto.com: Nosyrevy (cb/Crowd). 66 Alamy Stock Photo: Moviestore Collection Ltd (cla/King Creole); TCD / Prod.DB (cr); United Archives GmbH (bc); ZUMA Press, Inc (br). iStockphoto.com: Quirky Mundo (cla). 67 Alamy Stock Photo: DPA Picture Alliance (bc); Edd Westmacott (ca); WENN Rights Ltd (br). Getty Images: Kevin Winter / Getty Images for iHeartMedia (br). iStockphoto.com: Quirky Mundo (cl); Philartphace (clb). 68–69 Dreamstime.com: Alison Gibson (bc). 68 Alamy Stock Photo: Music Alan King (bc). Dreamstime.com: Alison Gibson (cl, tr); Ba–mi (cla). iStockphoto.com: Quirky Mundo (cla). 69 Alamy Stock Photo: Dmitry Nikolaev (tr). Dreamstime.com: Vadim Andreyev (br); Alison Gibson (tl, cra, cr, crb, cb); Siliconstudio (clb). Getty Images: Olly Curtis / Future Music Magazine / Future (c). iStockphoto.com: Quirky Mundo (b). Rex by Shutterstock: Joseph Branston / Future (cla). 70–71 Dreamstime.com: Alison Gibson. 70 Alamy Stock Photo: Andy Martin Jr (tc). Dreamstime.com: Alison Gibson (cb); Ba-mi (crb). Getty Images: Burak Cingi / Redferns (bc). 71 Alamy Stock Photo: Gonzales Photo (cla). Dreamstime.com: Alison Gibson (bc); Ryan Pike (tc); Orfeev (cr); Ilya Genkin / Igenkin (b). 72 Alamy Stock Photo: Agefotostock (cr); Herb Quick (cl); Pictorial Press Ltd (br). Dreamstime.com: Thomas Söllner (tl). Getty Images: PYMCA / Universal Images Group (bc). iStockphoto.com: Quirky Mundo (ca); Nosyrevy (cr/Crowd). 72–73 Alamy Stock Photo: Mark Azavedo (cb/Berlin Wall). Dreamstime.com: Alison Gibson (t, cb, b). 73 Alamy Stock Photo: Steve Black (bc); Edd Westmacott (br). Dreamstime.com: Davidtb (c); Thomas Söllner (tr). Getty Images: Helen Boast Photography / Redferns (cl). iStockphoto.com: Philartphace (tl). 74–75 Dreamstime.com: Alison Gibson. 74 Alamy Stock Photo: Frank Kahts Ethnic (bc). 75 Alamy Stock Photo: Cultura Creative (RF) (bc). Dreamstime.com: Alison Gibson (tr). iStockphoto.com: leonello (bl). 76–77 Dreamstime.com: Asrori Asrori; Alison Gibson (Circles). iStockphoto.com: Quirky Mundo (Background). 78–79 Dreamstime.com: Alison Gibson (t, cb, b). iStockphoto.com: Nosyrevy (cb/Crowd). 78 Alamy Stock Photo: Everett Collection Inc (cla). Dreamstime.com: Thomas Söllner (tl). iStockphoto.com: Quirky Mundo (cla). Rex by Shutterstock: (br); Yonhap / EPA (bc). 79 Alamy Stock Photo: Newscom (bc). Dreamstime.com: Michael Bush (cr); Thomas Söllner (tr). Getty Images: Ilgan Sports / Multi-Bits (cla); Mike Pont / WireImage (crb); RB / Bauer-Griffin / GC Images (br). iStockphoto.com: Quirky Mundo (Background). 80–81 iStockphoto.com: Quirky Mundo. 82–83 Dreamstime.com: Alison Gibson (t). iStockphoto.com: Wacomka (cb). 82 Alamy Stock Photo: Directphoto Collection (br); David Pearson (cra). Getty Images: Bettmann (bc); Rick Kern (c). iStockphoto.com: Quirky Mundo (cla). 83 Alamy Stock Photo: Anthony Brown (cra). Daniel Bollinger: (cla). Dreamstime.com: Tony Bosse (c); Pressureua (br). Getty Images: Bettmann (bc). 84 Dreamstime.com: Shane Cotee (clb). 84–85 Getty Images: English Heritage / Heritage Images; PamelaJoeMcFarlane (t). 85 Dreamstime.com: Alison Gibson (t). 86–87 Dreamstime.com: Alison Gibson. 86 Alamy Stock Photo: INTERFOTO (c); North Wind Picture Archives (cl). Getty Images: Paul Natkin (cr). 87 Getty Images: Petras Malukas / AFP (cra); Walter Daran / The LIFE Images Collection (cla); Gijsbert Hanekroot / Redferns (ca). 88–89 Dreamstime.com: Alison Gibson. 88 Dreamstime.com: Alison Gibson (tc). 89 Dreamstime.com: Alison Gibson (tl, b, tc, cr). 90–91 Dreamstime.com: Alison Gibson. 90 Alamy Stock Photo: Tjasa Janovljak (cb); Lebrecht Music & Arts (ca/Notation). Dorling Kindersley: Bate Collection (cb/Harpsichord). iStockphoto.com: Charnsitr (ca). The Metropolitan Museum of Art, New York: The Crosby Brown Collection of Musical Instruments, 1889 (cra). 91 Dreamstime.com: Iordanis Pallikaras (crb); Yury Shirokov (cr). Rex by Shutterstock: AP (cb); Joseph Branston / Future (ca). 92–93 Dreamstime.com: Alison Gibson. 94–95 Dreamstime.com: Alison Gibson. 95 Dreamstime.com: Alison Gibson (br). iStockphoto.com: Quirky Mundo (tc). 96 Dreamstime.com: Alison Gibson.

Endpaper images: Front: Dreamstime.com: Alison Gibson; Back: Dreamstime.com: Alison Gibson

Cover images: Front: Dreamstime.com: Alison Gibson (Background); iStockphoto.com: Bsd555 tc, cb; Back: 123RF.com: Gresel cl; Alamy Stock Photo: Judith Collins tc; Dorling Kindersley: Bate Collection tc/(B Flat Clarinet); Dreamstime.com: Alison Gibson (Background), Ba-mi cla; Spine: iStockphoto.com: Bsd555 t, b

All other images © Dorling Kindersley